Seth Anderson - Crork

Motive power recognition: 4
LONDON TRANSPORT
RAILWAYS
and PTE Systems

John Glover & Colin J. Marsden

LONDON

IAN ALLAN LTD

First published 1985

ISBN 0 7110 1460 4

© Ian Allan Ltd 1985

Published by Ian Allan Ltd, Shepperton, Surrey;
and printed by Ian Allan Printing Ltd at their works
at Coombelands in Runnymede, England

Front cover: 'D' stock at Ealing Common
depot in 1983. *Alan Butcher*

Back cover: Tyne & Wear Metro system
set No 4082 bound for St. James.
Colin J. Marsden

Below: A six-car train of District line
stock departs from Wimbledon with a
Tower Hill service on 10 April 1981.
The section of line from Wimbledon to
Putney Bridge is owned by BR with LT
operating powers and the portion
between Wimbledon and East Putney
has timetabled BR services, usually in
the form of empty EMU trains to and
from East Wimbledon car depot.
Colin J. Marsden

Introduction

There are more than 4,000 passenger cars running on the Underground system of London Regional Transport, many of which are of similar appearance to the uninitiated. There are two principal sub-divisions, that of the larger sub-surface stock built for the cut and cover lines of the Metropolitan, Circle and District, and the tube stock constructed for the deep level lines with bored tunnels beneath the capital. Although differing in dimensions, all stock shares a common electrical system of fourth rail 600 volts dc.

The first part of this fourth volume in the *Motive Power Recognition* series provides a general introduction to the London Underground system, followed by a brief description of each line. Car types are closely identified with the lines on which they work. Variations in platform lengths, clearances on curves, and equipment for Driver Only Operation are some of the reasons why stock is not as interchangeable between lines as might be thought. Each type of car is described in detail. Supporting the passenger cars is a substantial fleet of service stock ranging from electric, diesel and battery locomotives, through service vehicles converted from older Underground cars, to a specialised wagon stock for engineering duties throughout the system.

Each vehicle is numbered separately and there are no unit numbers, although the car numbers in a unit's formation often relate. Thus the car numbers of the first of the 1972 Mk I four-car units are, successively, 3201-4201-4301-3301, and this sequence continues through all 39 such sets. Livery for all postwar passenger vehicles is unpainted aluminium, with lettering and sometimes doors or a panel below the driver's windows picked out in red. Red livery will become extinct with the withdrawal of the last of the '1938' tube stock. Internal finishes vary, but recent stock has displayed a much more prominent use of bright colours than earlier builds. Service stock is in an all-over highly visible yellow livery, which is replacing the previous maroon.

Some other systems have also been included: the Isle of Wight with its former London Transport stock, together with British Rail's Waterloo & City line, Strathclyde's Glasgow Underground system, the Tyne & Wear Metro and the Docklands Light Railway in London. All of the latter are (or will be) rapid transit systems in their own right. A final section takes a look at London Transport stock in preservation.

We would like to thank all those who have provided photographs for this book, especially of the more obscure items. Details of rolling stock changes and much other information are published in *Underground News,* the journal of the London Underground Railway Society. Membership of this Society is recommended to all those interested in the railways covered in this volume.

The Editors would like to hear of any major detail differences or features which have not been covered in this book. Please send any information, accompanied by a photograph if available to: The Editors, Motive Power Recognition, Ian Allan Ltd, Terminal House, Shepperton, TW17 8AS.

During the production of this book, the London Regional Transport Act transferred control of the London Transport Executive from the GLC to Central Government. As a consequence LTE is now officially known as LRT. However, references to LT and LTE have been left unchanged within this book.

John Glover/Colin J. Marsden
October 1984

Right: Front end comparisons of various LT stock, from front to back. Electric Sleet Loco No ESL 117 (converted from 1903 Central London Railway driving cars); Battery loco No 32 built in 1964 by Metro-Cammell; a train of '1938' tube stock, and at the rear the leading end of ESL 118A/B a converted set of 'T' stock introduced in 1961.
John Glover

London Transport
Organisation and Staff

London Transport – now renamed London Regional Transport – is the authority responsible for the control and operation of London's Underground and Bus services. Its headquarters are at 55 Broadway, London SW1. The LRT board consists of a Chairman, Deputy Chairman, Managing Directors for the bus and rail businesses, and eight other part time members. Reporting to the Managing Director, Railways, and responsible for the day to day running of the Underground, are four Divisional General Managers. Their responsibilities are for:

(i)   Metropolitan, Jubilee and Circle Lines
(ii)   Northern and Victoria Lines
(iii)   District and Piccadilly Lines
(iv)   Central and Bakerloo Lines

A General Manager has also been appointed for the Docklands Light Railway project. There are some 23,900 staff on the Underground, as follows:

Motormen and Guards	4,000
Traffic Control	7,100
Engineering	12,200
Police	300
Business Administration	300
Total	*23,900*

Below: There are a number of locations on the LT system where trains of different types can be captured on film together, thus clearly showing the recognition differences between them. This illustration taken at Finchley Central shows '1959' stock on the left and 1972 Mk I stock on the right. Both trains are operating on the Northern Line and it is interesting to note that both are showing incorrect destination blinds opposite to the direction in which they are travelling. *John Glover*

Passengers

Passenger usage of the system can be measured either in terms of the number of journeys made or the total mileage covered by passengers, which takes journey length into account. The number of journeys stated includes those starting or finishing their journey on British Rail. All figures relate to 1983.

Passengers carried	563 million
Passenger miles	2,700 million
Average journey length	4.8 miles
Number of passengers carried daily (Monday–Friday average)	1,830,000
Average passenger load per train	94

System

The extent of the system can be measured in terms of either single track miles or as route miles, ie irrespective of the number of individual tracks. British Rail tracks are used in a few instances, such as the Bakerloo Line between Queen's Park and Harrow & Wealdstone.

Length of single track open for traffic (miles)

Running Lines	519
Sidings	159
Total single track miles	*678*

Below: People are not usually aware of the difference in size between 'tube' and 'surface' stock but this illustration taken at Rayners Lane clearly shows the size differences. On the left is a train of 1973 stock operating a Piccadilly line service to Arnos Grove, whilst on the right stands a train of 'A60' surface stock on a Metropolitan line service to Uxbridge. *Colin J. Marsden*

Length of route miles managed by London Transport (miles)

Single track	12
Double track	207
Triple track	3
Quadruple or more tracks	19
	241
Length of British Rail route run over	13
Total system route miles	*254*

A minority of the system is in tunnel. Generally, the 'surface' lines (Metropolitan, District and Circle) were constructed by the cut and cover method, while the deep level tubes are in bored tunnels.

Length of route in tunnel (miles)

Cut and cover	20
Tube	82
Total route miles in tunnel	*102* representing 40% of total route miles

Average depth of tunnel sections below ground (ft)

'sub-surface'	24ft
'tube'	80ft

Above: This panoramic view shows Ealing Broadway station where the District and Central lines meet. Although the two lines are operated completely separately, there is an inter-connection which can clearly be seen in this picture. On the left a train of 'D' stock arrives with a District line train from Upminster, whilst on the right 1962 stock arrives in the Central line platforms with a service from Hainault. In the background a withdrawn set of 'CO/CP' stock can be seen in the sidings. *John Glover*

Inter-connection between lines, not normally used for passenger traffic

Lines are automatically connected with each other where they share the same pair of tracks (for example District and Piccadilly Lines at Ealing Common), and connections are provided where lines run parallel in the open (for example Metropolitan and Jubilee Lines between Finchley Road and Wembley Park). Connections between lines are essential to permit the movement of stock around the system, notably to and from Acton Works, and to allow operation of engineering trains. Other connections are:

Between (lines)	Location	Direction (facing connections unless shown)
Metropolitan/District and East London	Whitechapel (St Mary's Curve)	Eastbound Metropolitan/District to Southbound East London. Northbound East London to Westbound Metropolitan/District
Northern (City) and Piccadilly	King's Cross	Northbound Northern City and Eastbound Piccadilly. Single track, both trailing connections. Crossover provided on Piccadilly, reversing facilities available at Euston, Northern Line
Piccadilly and Victoria	Finsbury Park	Northbound Piccadilly to Northbound Victoria. Southbound Victoria to Southbound Piccadilly
Jubilee and Bakerloo	Baker Street	Northbound Bakerloo to Northbound Jubilee. Southbound Jubilee to Southbound Bakerloo
District and Central	Ealing Broadway	Siding connection
Metropolitan/Piccadilly and Central	Ruislip	Depot access to both lines

There are also a limited number of connections to British Rail lines.

Trains

Apart from the few services which are provided at all times by 3/4 coach trains, for example Holborn–Aldwych, train lengths are standardised at six, seven or eight cars according to the rolling stock and the line on which used. The practice of reducing train lengths at off peak times has been abandoned.

Train miles run over London Transport tracks	28,659,327
Train miles run over British Rail tracks	362,979
Total train miles (1982)	*29,022,306*
Average scheduled train speed	20.5 mile/h

Rolling stock owned	
Underground cars-motor	2,630
Underground cars-trailer	1,439
Total cars owned	*4,069*

Stations

The busiest Underground stations are all in central London, though the usage quoted takes no account of passenger interchange between lines, as opposed to those entering or leaving the premises.

Number of stations served:
Managed by London Transport	247
Managed by British Rail	24
Total stations served	*271*

Busiest stations by passengers starting and ending journeys (excluding interchange)

Station	Numbers (millions)	Lines served
Victoria	48m	District, Circle, Victoria
Oxford Circus	39m	Bakerloo, Central, Victoria
Liverpool Street	31m	Metropolitan, Circle, Central
King's Cross	30m	Metropolitan, Circle, Northern, Piccadilly, Victoria
Waterloo	25m	Bakerloo, Northern
Piccadilly Circus	22m	Bakerloo, Piccadilly
Stations serving most lines:		King's Cross (5)

Stations with most platforms:
Baker Street (10):   4 Metropolitan main, 2 Hammersmith & City/Circle, 2 Bakerloo, 2 Jubilee
Moorgate (10):   2 Northern, 4 Metropolitan/Circle, 2 Midland Suburban, 2 Great Northern Suburban

Stations on single lines with only one platform do not necessarily have a limited service. When Heathrow Terminal 4 opens, it will be served by all trains using that branch of the Piccadilly Line.

Stations with only one platform in operational use by London Transport trains:

Aldwych	New Cross Gate
Chesham	North Weald
Kensington Olympia	Ongar
Mill Hill East	Shoreditch
New Cross	Heathrow Terminal 4 (under construction)

Left: A station at Harrow-on-the-Hill was opened on 2 August 1880 as the Western terminus of the Metropolitan Railway, named Harrow, it remained so until June 1894 when it was renamed Harrow-on-the-Hill, a year before the line was extended on towards Pinner. In this 1983 view of the station 'A62' stock arrives led by DM No 5204 on a train bound for Baker Street.
Colin J. Marsden .

Above: Of the 271 stations on the London Transport system the most difficult to photograph are those underground, mainly situated in the Central London area. Pulling into the modernised Charing Cross station, first opened to the public on 22 June 1907, is a train of '1959' stock forming a Northern Line Morden–High Barnet service on 13 April 1983. Charing Cross station was renamed Strand in 1915 but returned to its original name in 1979 when a new intersection with the Jubilee line was opened. *John Glover*

Below: There are few sections of single line operation on LT, but the Central line between Epping and Ongar has had a single track since its opening as part of the GER on 24 April 1865. Today the section only opens during peak hours when a shuttle service operates. A 4-car formation of '1962' stock is used and when photographed at Ongar in 1981 DM No 1593 was leading. *Brian Morrison*

Vertical transport

Access to tunnel sections of the Underground may be by lifts, escalators or stairs. Lifts have the disadvantage in that service cannot be continuous, whereas escalators allow for a constant stream of passengers. At the deepest stations such as Hampstead, the speed of the lift offsets the disadvantage of having to wait for it. Most central area stations were constructed before the escalator was introduced; those that are now so equipped underwent extensive rebuilding. The use of escalators is not confined to the tunnel sections of the system.

Lifts

First lift installed	All stations King William Street–Stockwell, 1890
Number of stations with lifts	26
Number of lifts	69
Average speed, standard lift	180ft/min
Average speed, high speed automatic lifts	500–800ft/min
Deepest lift shaft	Hampstead, 181ft
Shallowest lift shaft	Chalk Farm, 30ft 6in
Lifts incorporating ticket office	Aldwych, Mornington Crescent

Escalators

First escalator installed	Earl's Court, 1911
Number of stations with escalators	69
Number of escalators	273
Longest escalator	Leicester Squre, 161ft slope
Shortest escalator	Chancery Lane, 30ft slope
Average length of escalators on slope	88ft
Average vertical rise of escalators	44ft
Average number of steps	188
Service speed	90–145ft/min
Station with most escalators	Oxford Circus (14)
Station with most escalators in one shaft	Holborn (4)
Stations with platforms above ground level and escalators	Alperton, Greenford

Left: The 'Vertical Transport' at Earls Court illustrates the exhibition subway escalators and central stairway. Emergency push buttons to stop the escalators are seen at the base of the escalators. Ceiling faced lighting provides illumination by reflection on the white roof. The advertising frames at this station usually carry relevant advertising of products in association with exhibitions being staged at the adjacent centre. *John Glover*

Electricity supply

The Underground is operated throughout on 600 volts dc, fourth rail. Most of the power comes from London Transport's own generating stations.

Generating stations	Installed capacity (MW)	Fuel consumption 1981 (thousand therms)
Lots Road, Chelsea	180	4,764 (low distillate oil)
		65,606 (natural gas)
Greenwich Gas Turbine Plant	118	1,317 (low distillate oil)
		12,582 (natural gas)

Total units used for London Transport services 866 million, including units purchased

Number of traction substations	114
Substation output voltage	630v dc
Nominal track voltage	600v dc

Below: General view of the Victoria line control room at Cobourg Street, with the operator in the foreground and the track diagram on the wall behind, Walthamstow Central being on the far left and Warren Street on the right. *LTE*

Acton Works

London Transport has one major undertaking responsible for the classified repairs and maintenance of all its railborne stock — Acton Works. The complex covers 50 acres and was built simultaneously with Chiswick works — responsible for bus repairs, during 1922. The two premises are separated by a railway line.

Underground trains are usually overhauled every 5–10 years, depending on stock type, age and general condition. When vehicles are called to works, mileage covered since their last visit can be anything between 250,000–600,000 miles. The works is operated on a 'flow-line' system, where vehicles progress along the shop as repairs are carried out. The works includes the following main buildings — Apprentice Training Centre, Motor Shop, Trimming Shop, Car Lifting Shop, Repair Shop, Car Body Shop, Smith's Truck and Wheel Shop and Heavy Duty Shop. Two traversers connect with siding lines feeding the various shops enabling stock to be moved as and when required.

Above: Standing on the traverser outside one of Acton's workshops, is car No 1576 which is a Driving Motor 'A' end vehicle of '1962' Central line stock. The traverser can move vehicles between bays in a sideways movement. Access on and off of the traverser is usually effected by means of a capstan and rope. *John Glover*

Above: When vehicles undergo repairs at Acton works they are often mounted on accommodation bogies enabling them to be placed high off the ground for underside maintenance. Vehicles can also be easily moved around the works as the classified overhaul procedure uses the 'flow line' system. Mounted on accommodation bogies is 1972 Mk II DM No 3238, from a four-car unit. Note the radio link aerial on the car front. *John Glover*

Below: Three battery locomotives Nos 51, 24 and 48 stand inside one of the main works buildings at Acton during July 1983. Locomotive No 51 built in 1974 by BREL Doncaster Works, has its buffers extended, while Nos 24 and 48, a Metro-Cammell and BREL Doncaster-built loco have their buffers folded away. *John Glover*

Metropolitan main line

Baker Street (Aldgate in peak hours) to Amersham, with branches to Chesham, Watford and Uxbridge.
Line category: Surface.
Route miles: 41.
Number of stations served: 34.
Number of trains required to operate service:
    in peak hours, **Monday to Friday:** 39x8car, 1x4car
    in off peak, **Monday to Friday:** 15x8car, 1x4car
    on **Saturday:** 13x8car, 1x4car
    on **Sunday:** 13x8car, 1x4car
    Note: 1x4car train is used on the Chesham branch.
Rolling stock type: 'A' stock.
Main depot: Neasden.
Minor depot: Wembley Park.
Sidings: Rickmansworth, Uxbridge and Watford.
Oldest section: Baker Street–Swiss Cottage (station closed), opened 1868; (in town section Baker Street–Farringdon opened 1863).
Section in tunnel: Aldgate–Finchley Road, mostly cut and cover construction with open air sections. Bored tunnel between Moor Park and Croxley.
System records
Farthest west: Amersham, Buckinghamshire, 27 miles from central London.
Longest distance between adjacent stations: Chalfont and Latimer–Chesham, 3.89 miles.
Highest station above mean sea level: Amersham, 490ft.
Largest car park: Wembley Park, 634 spaces.
Last use of steam and electric locomotives in regular passenger service: 1961.
Last use of steam locomotives on Underground: 1971.

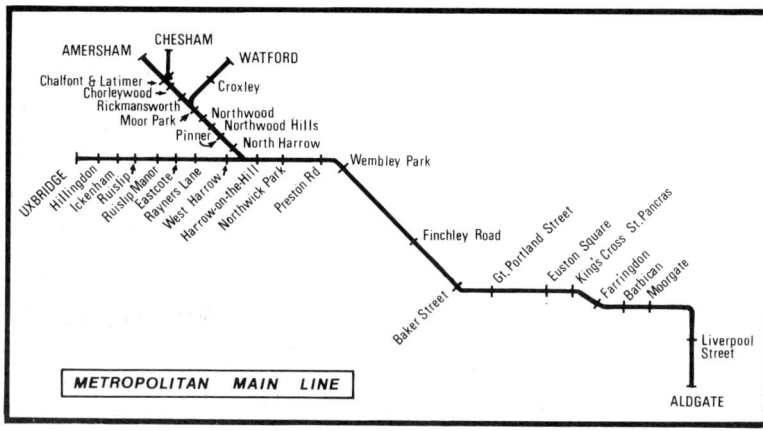

Below: The 41 route miles of the Metropolitan main line, between Baker Street and Amersham, Chesham, Watford and Uxbridge is served by 'A60' and 'A62' stock, normally formed into eight-car sets, made up of two four-car formations. 'A62' set with DM 'D' south car No 5221 leading, approaches West Hampstead on a train bound for Wembley Park. *John Glover*

Bottom: One of the major intersections on the Metropolitan main line is Harrow-on-the-Hill, where the route to Uxbridge parts company from the lines to Amersham, Chesham and Watford. A train of 'A' stock approaches Harrow-on-the-Hill station from Uxbridge during the summer of 1983. *Colin J. Marsden*

Metropolitan East London line

Whitechapel (Shoreditch in peak hours and Sunday mornings) to New Cross and New Cross Gate.

Line category: Sub-surface.
Route miles: 5.
Number of stations served: 8.
   of which, British Rail owned: 2 (New Cross and New Cross Gate).
Number of trains required to operate service:
   in peak hours, Monday to Friday: 5x4car
   In off peak, Monday to Friday: 3x4car
   on Saturday: 3x4car
   on Sunday: 3x4car.
Rolling stock type: 'A' stock.
Depot: New Cross.
Oldest section: The Thames Tunnel (Wapping–Rotherhithe) was opened to public pedestrian traffic in 1843. Purchased by the East London Railway, it was closed in 1869, but reopened for rail traffic later the same year. Worked initially by the London, Brighton & South Coast Railway, it became part of the Underground in 1884, although no underground trains ran in the period 1906–13.
Section in tunnel: Whitechapel (exc)–Surrey Docks (exc).
System records
Maximum depth of sub surface line below ground level: Wapping, 60ft.
Oldest section of tunnel used by London Transport trains: Between Wapping and Rotherhithe, 1843.

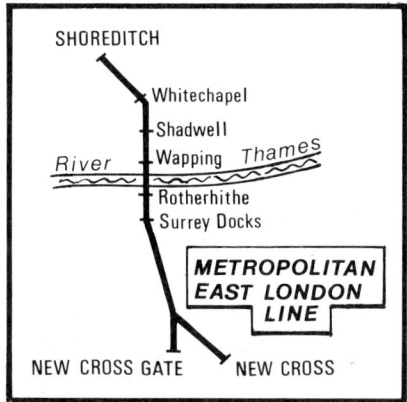

Left: Another section of the Metropolitan line is entitled the 'East London line' operating between Shoreditch–New Cross and New Cross Gate. Trains used on this section are formed of only four-car sets. Pulling into Shadwell station and under a screen protecting the track/trains from rubbish thrown from above properties, is a train of 'A' stock forming the shuttle service from Whitechapel to New Cross.
John Glover

Left: The 'East London Line' became part of the Underground in October 1884, although it was not served by Underground trains between 1906 and 1913, from which date it was electrified. Approaching Wapping, where the line is some 60ft below ground level, a set of 'A' stock forms a train to Whitechapel, emerging into the light of the station after passing deep under the Thames. *John Glover*

Below: The section between Whitechapel and Surrey Docks is of square tunnel section (just below surface), with the two branches to New Cross/New Cross Gate being overground lines. Departing from Surrey Docks, a four-car train of 'A' stock forms a service to New Cross Gate during 1980. The station buildings at this location have now been completely rebuilt. *John Glover*

District line, main (excluding Edgware Road–Wimbledon)

Between Upminster and Ealing Broadway, with branches to Richmond, Wimbledon and Kensington (Olympia).
Line type: Sub-surface.
Route miles: 37.
Number of stations served: 55.
  of which, British Rail owned: 11 (Ealing Broadway, Richmond–Gunnersbury, Wimbledon–East Putney, Kensington (Olympia), Barking and Upminster).
  Note: East Putney, Southfields, Wimbledon Park and Wimbledon have no regular British Rail passenger service over these tracks.
Number of trains required to operate service:
  in peak hours, Monday to Friday: 59x6car
  in off peak, Monday to Friday: 37x6car
  on Saturday: 25x6car
  on Sunday: 18x6car.
Note: Two additional trains are required whenever the Olympia exhibition service is in operation.
Rolling stock type: 'D' stock.
Main depot: Ealing Common.
Subsidiary depot: Upminster.
Sidings: Parsons Green and Barking.
Platform storage: High Street, Kensington.
Oldest Section: Edgware Road–Gloucester Road, and then Westminster. Opened 1868, but worked originally by the Metropolitan.
Sections in tunnel: Bow Road–West Brompton/West Kensington. All in cut and cover construction, with several short sections and stations in open air eg Sloane Square. Bored tunnel between East Putney and Southfields.
System records
Furthest east: Upminster, 18 miles from central London.
Most frequent service: Tower Hill–Gloucester Road, 31 trains per hour in evening peak.
First trial application of automatic train operation: Between Stamford Brook and Ravenscourt Park, 1962.
Last use of semaphore signalling by Underground trains: Richmond, 1980.

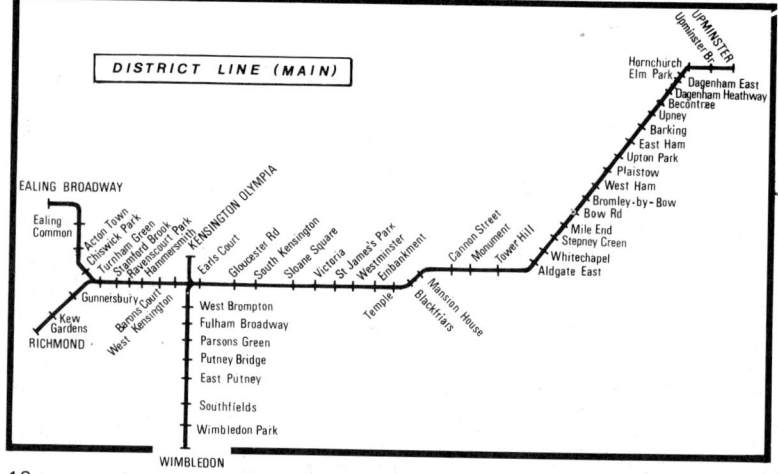

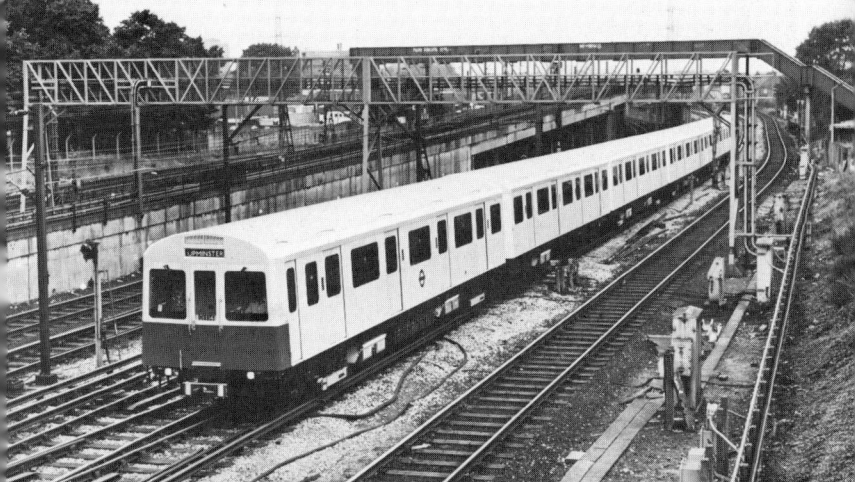

Above: The District line (main) is basically an arterial East–West route between Upminster and Ealing Broadway, with branches at the west end to Richmond, Wimbledon and Kensington Olympia. The total route mileage is 37, and stock of 'D' types is used. Standing at Earls Court with a Kensington Olympia–High Street Kensington exhibition service, a train of 'D' stock has DM No 7009 leading. *John Glover*

Below: Both BR and London Transport tracks come side by side at Barking, where the District/Metropolitan lines run adjacent to the Barking–Gospel Oak and London–Shoeburyness BR routes. Approaching the station and passing Barking flyover, a train of 'D' stock led by DM No 7065 forms a service from Wimbledon to Upminster on 8 August 1981. *Colin J. Marsden*

Circle Line

A combination of the central sections of the Metropolitan and District Lines, connecting most of London's main line railway termini. Technically, part of the Metropolitan Line.

Hammersmith & City (Metropolitan)

Hammersmith to Whitechapel, with a peak hour only extension to Barking.

Edgware Road–Wimbledon (District Line)

A separately operated part of the District Line.

These three lines are considered together, since they share many facilities and form the complete operating area of the C stock.
Line type: Sub-surface.
Route miles: 31.
Number of stations served: 47.
 of which, British Rail owned: 4 (Wimbledon–East Putney).
Number of trains required to operate service (all six car sets).

	Circle	Hammersmith & City	Edgware Road– Wimbledon
Monday to Friday peak hours	14	16	7
Monday to Friday, off peak	14	11	4
Saturday	10	8	7
Sunday	10	8	4

Rolling stock type: 'C' stock.
Main depot: Hammersmith.
Subsidiary depot: Neasden.
Minor depot: Triangle Sidings, Cromwell Curve.
Sidings: Farringdon, Barking and Parsons Green.
Platform storage: Aldgate, Edgware Road and Moorgate.
Oldest sections: Circle: Throughout service inaugurated 1884.
 Hammersmith & City: Baker Street–Farringdon, opened 1863.
 Edgware Road–Wimbledon: Edgware Road–High Street Kensington (Gloucester Road), opened 1868 and operated by Metropolitan.
Sections in tunnel: All in cut and cover construction, apart from open air sections Hammersmith–Paddington, Bow Road–Barking, and West Brompton–Wimbledon. Bored tunnel between East Putney and Southfields.

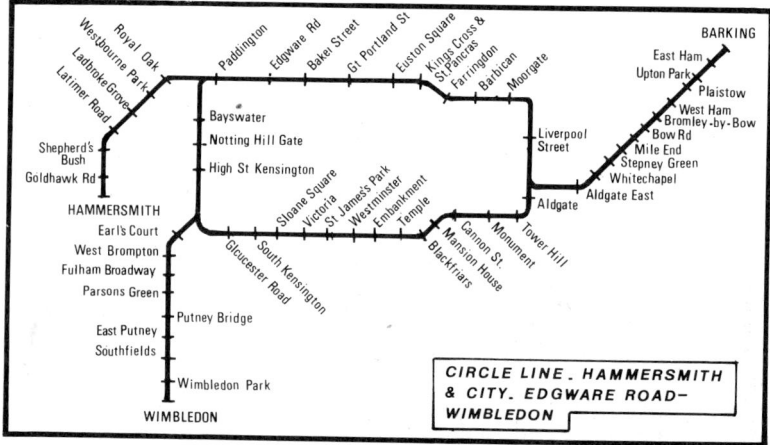

CIRCLE LINE. HAMMERSMITH & CITY. EDGWARE ROAD–WIMBLEDON

Cut and cover results in several short open sections and stations, notably at Whitechapel, between King's Cross and Barbican, and in the Kensington area.

System records

First Underground railway: Baker Street–Farringdon opened 10 January 1863, built as mixed gauge line and operated initially by the Great Western Railway with broad gauge rolling stock.

Introduction of opo (one person operation): Hammersmith & City Line, 1984.

Above: A typical London Transport scene, a crowded station of passengers awaiting their rapid transit service. A train of 'C' stock arrives at Mansion House on the Circle line whilst working a clockwise service. All DM cars operating on the Circle line are fitted with radio link equipment. *John Glover*

Left: The Wimbledon spur of the District line diverges from the main route at Earls Court. In addition to operating on the Circle line 'C' stock is used on some duties on the Wimbledon branch, usually on Edgware Road services. Pulling into Earls Court on 4 June 1980 a six car formation of 'C' stock is seen en route from Wimbledon to Edgware Road. *John Glover*

Bakerloo Line

From Elephant & Castle to Queens Park, with peak hour extension to Harrow & Wealdstone.
Line type: Tube.
Route miles: 14.
Number of stations served: 25.
    of which, British Rail owned: 10 (Queens Park–Harrow & Wealdstone).
Number of trains required to operate service:
    in peak hours, Monday–Friday; 25x7car
    in off peak, Monday–Friday: 17x7car
    on Saturday: 11x7car
    on Sunday: 9x7car.

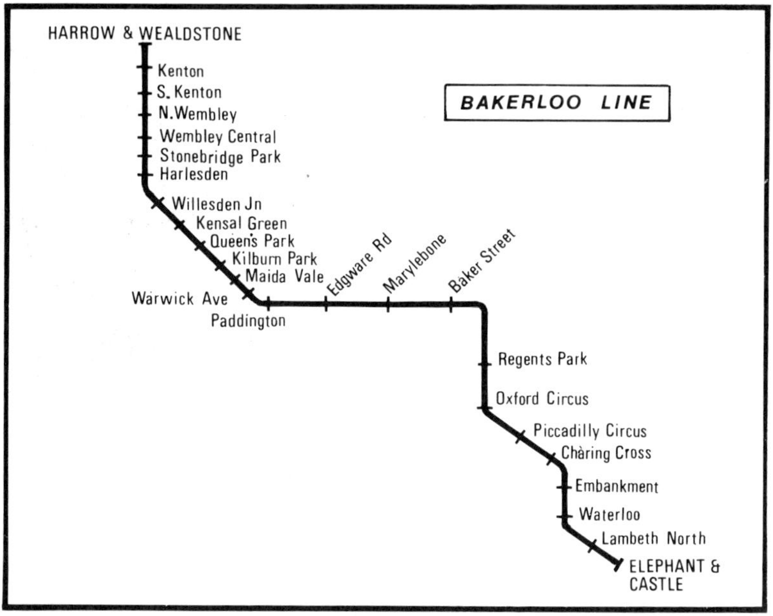

HARROW & WEALDSTONE

Kenton
S. Kenton
N. Wembley
Wembley Central
Stonebridge Park
Harlesden
Willesden Jn
Kensal Green
Queen's Park
Kilburn Park
Maida Vale
Warwick Ave
Paddington
Edgware Rd
Marylebone
Baker Street

BAKERLOO LINE

Regents Park
Oxford Circus
Piccadilly Circus
Charing Cross
Embankment
Waterloo
Lambeth North
ELEPHANT & CASTLE

Left: The Bakerloo line will soon be operated entirely by '1959' type tube stock; however for many years until 1985 the line was host to the red liveried 1938 tube stock, formed into seven-car formations. Two trains of this distinctive stock pass at Piccadilly Circus during 1983, the interchange point with the Piccadilly line.
John Glover

Rolling stock type: '1938' and '1959' stock.
Main depot: Stonebridge Park.
Subsidiary depot: Queens Park.
Minor depot: London Road.
Siding: Elephant & Castle.
Oldest section: Baker Street–Lambeth North, opened 1906.
Section in tunnel: Queens Park (exc)–Elephant & Castle (inc).

Above: The southern end of the Bakerloo line terminates at Elephant & Castle. Between Lambeth North and Elephant & Castle stations lies London Road depot, which provides accommodation and maintenance for some of the Bakerloo line stock, the main depot being at Stonebridge Park. A train of '1959' stock arrives at London Road depot on 10 June 1983 for overnight stabling, after operating peak hour services. *John Glover*

Below: A number of platforms on various tube lines have been refurbished in recent years with tiled walls, improved lighting and fixed seating. A train of '1959' stock pulls into Baker Street Bakerloo line southbound platform. Note the route map on the tunnel wall (left) and the direction indicator for Jubilee line passengers hanging from the roof (right). *John Glover*

Central Line

Ealing Broadway and West Ruislip to Hainault and Epping, with a peak hour branch to Ongar, and a loop from Woodford to Hainault.

Line type: Tube.
Route miles: 52.
Number of stations served: 51.
   of which, British Rail owned: 2 (Ealing Broadway, Stratford).
Number of trains required to operate service:
   in peak hours, Monday to Friday: 71x8car; 2x3car; 1x4car
   in off peak, Monday–Friday: 40x8car; 2x3car
   on Saturday: 30x8car; 1x3car
   on Sunday: 27x8car; 1x3car.
Note: 3car units are used on the Woodford–Hainault service, 1x4car unit on the Epping–Ongar branch.
Rolling stock types: '1962' stock; Woodford–Hainault service operated by Automatic Train Operation (ATO) fitted '1960' and '1973' stock.
Main depot: West Ruislip.
Subsidiary depot: Hainault.
Minor depot: White City.
Sidings: Loughton, Woodford and West Ruislip.
Oldest section: Shepherd's Bush–Bank, opened 1900.
Sections in tunnel: White City (exc)–Stratford (exc), Stratford (exc)–Leyton (exc), Leytonstone (exc)–Newbury Park (exc), and between Grange Park and Chigwell.
Station with right hand running: White City.
System records
Longest possible journey without change: West Ruislip–Epping, 34.1 miles.
Furthest north: Ongar, Essex, 24 miles from central London.
Use of locomotives on tube line: From opening in 1900 until 1903.

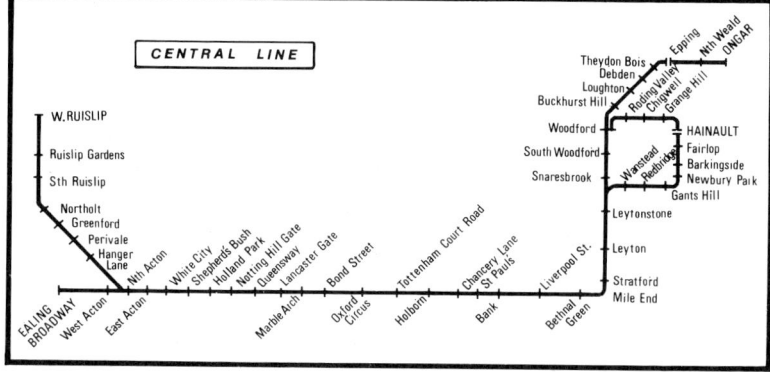

Above: The longest LT line is the Central running on a basic west–east axis from Ealing Broadway/West Ruislip to Hainault/Epping. The line uses '1962' stock for all services except ATO fitted 1960 and ETT 1973 stock on the Woodford–Hainault shuttle. Pulling into Bank station an eastbound service is captured on film on 13 September 1983 with DM No 1699 leading. This station provides interconnection with the Northern line and the BR operated Waterloo & City Railway. *John Glover*

Left: The section of the Central line between Woodford and Hainault is often used for experimental purposes and for a number of years has been the host to 1960 stock fitted with automatic train operation (ATO) equipment. A three-car set with Cravens built DM cars approaches Grange Hill with a Woodford train on 19 March 1982. *John Glover*

Jubilee Line

Charing Cross to Stanmore.
Line type: Tube.
Route miles: 14.
Number of stations served: 17.
Number of trains required to operate service:
 in peak hours, Monday to Friday: 23x6/7car.
 in off peak, Monday to Friday: 16x6/7car
 on Saturday: 13x6/7car.
 on Sunday: 8x6/7car.
Rolling stock types: 7car '1972' Mark II stock, 6car '1983' stock.
Main depot: Neasden.
Minor depot: Stanmore.
Oldest section: Wembley Park–Stanmore, opened 1932 as branch of Metropolitan Line.
Transferred to Bakerloo Line 1939 and Jubilee Line 1979.
Section in tunnel: Finchley Road (exc)–Charing Cross (inc).
Station with right hand running: Baker Street.

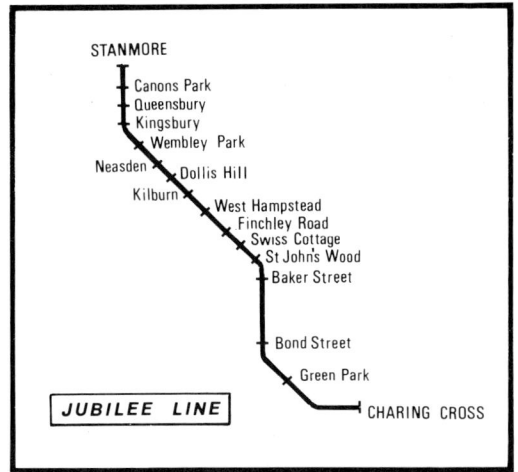

Above: The 14-mile long Jubilee line is the newest addition to the LTE network, commencing full
operation in 1979. However the only actual 'new' section was between Charing Cross and Baker Street,
some 2.55 miles, the remainder being taken over from the Bakerloo line. Approaching the joint
Metropolitan/Jubilee station of Wembley Park is a train of '1972' Mk II stock on 20 October 1983.
Colin J. Marsden

Above: The depot at Neasden is responsible for maintenance of Jubilee line stock, minor maintenance and stabling being carried out additionally at Stanmore. Inside the lifting shop at Neasden on 24 April 1983 is a DM of a '1972' Mk II set; note the motor bogie in front. *John Glover*

Below: On weekdays during peak periods a total of 23 units are needed to fully operate the advertised passenger service, however Sunday services are less frequent and only eight trains are required. '1972' Mk II stock approaches West Hampstead on 16 September 1978 with a Stanmore service, when the line was still under the Bakerloo flag. *Brian Morrison*

Northern Line

Morden to Edgware, Mill Hill East or High Barnet, via Bank or Charing Cross.
Line type: Tube.
Route miles: 36.
Number of stations served: 49.
Number of trains required to operate service:
    in peak hours, Monday to Friday: 82x7car
    in off peak, Monday to Friday: 46x7car
    on Saturday: 36x7car
    on Sunday: 36x7car.
Rolling stock types: '1956' (prototype); '1959'; '1962'; '1972' Mark I; '1972' Mark II.
Main depot: Golders Green.
Subsidiary depot: Morden.
Minor depot: Edgware.
Sidings: Golders Green, High Barnet.
Oldest section: King William Street (closed)–Borough–Stockwell, opened 1890.
Sections in tunnel: East Finchley (exc)/Golders Green (exc)–Morden (exc) via both Charing Cross and Bank; Between Hendon Central and Colindale.
Stations with right hand running: Bank and London Bridge.
Station with terminal loop: Kennington.
System records
Furthest south: Morden, 10 miles from central London.
Longest continuous tunnel: East Finchley–Morden via Bank, 17 miles 528yds.

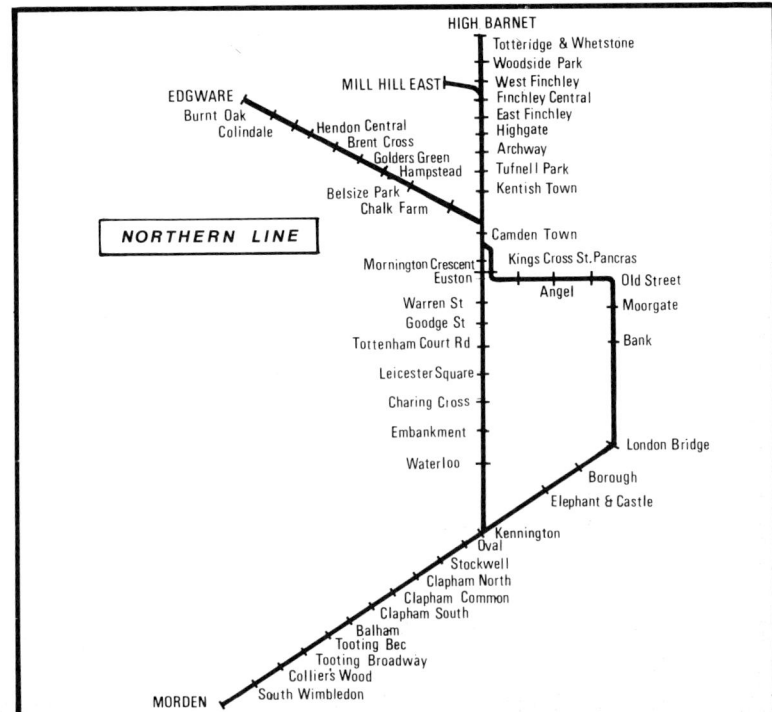

Maximum depth below ground level: At Holly Bush Hill, Hampstead, 221ft.
Maximum depth below mean sea level: South of Waterloo, 70ft.
Deepest station: Hampstead, 181ft.
Greatest elevation from ground level: Dollis Brook Viaduct, over Dollis Road, Mill Hill East branch, 60ft.

Above: A general view of Golders Green car sidings on the Northern line, showing a mixture of 1972 and now redundant '1938' stock side by side. Two electric sleet locomotives and a pair of ballast motor cars are also visible. Behind the photographer the lines converge into a shunting neck which is a tunnel parallel to the running line, and from where access can be gained to the running lines. *LTE*

Left: The Mill Hill East branch diverges from the High Barnet line at Finchley Central. Prior to reaching Mill Hill East station trains travel over the Dollis Brook Viaduct, carrying the line across Dollis Road, and at this point the Northern line is at its highest point above ground level—60ft. A train of '1959' stock is seen on the viaduct during September 1978.
John Glover

Piccadilly Line

Cockfosters to Heathrow Terminals 1, 2 and 3 or Uxbridge, with a peak hour shuttle service between Holborn and Aldwych.

Line type: Tube.
Route miles: 40.
Number of stations served: 51.
Number of trains required to operate service:
    in peak hours, Monday to Friday: 70x6car; 1x3car
    in off peak, Monday to Friday: 46x6car
    on Saturday: 39x6car.
    on Sunday: 28x6car.
Note: 1x3car unit operates on Aldwych branch.
Rolling stock type: '1973' stock.

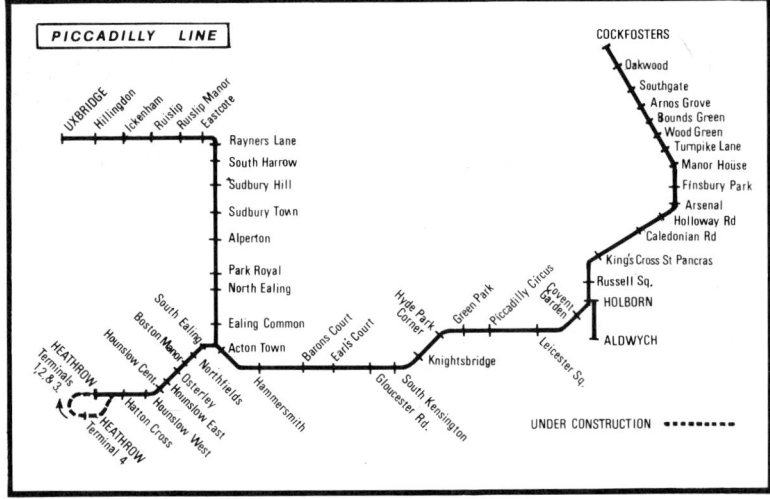

Left: Apart from one three-car set operating on the Central line as the ETT, all '1973' stock operates on the Piccadilly line, which during peak periods requires some 60 six-car sets to provide the full passenger service. The most important function of this line is to provide a connection between the centre of London and Heathrow Airport a service which became fully operational in December 1977. Passing fast through Turnham Green station a Piccadilly line train forms a service for Heathrow during October 1983.
Colin J. Marsden

Main depot: Northfields.
Subsidiary depot: Cockfosters.
Sidings: South Harrow, Arnos Grove and Uxbridge.
Oldest section: Finsbury Park–Hammersmith, opened 1906.
Sections in tunnel: Arnos Grove (exc)–Barons Court (exc), including Aldwych branch; Hounslow West (inc)–Heathrow Terminals 1, 2 and 3 (inc) (short surface section between Hounslow West and Hatton Cross), and at Southgate.
System records
Shortest distance between two adjacent stations: Leicester Square–Covent Garden, 0.16 miles.
Stations designated as of special architectural interest: Oakwood, Southgate, Arnos Grove and Sudbury Town.
Section under construction: Hatton Cross–Heathrow Terminal 4–Heathrow Terminals 1, 2 and 3 (single track loop).

Above: Although the Piccadilly line traverses the same route as the District line between Earls Court and Acton Town, services do not call at all stations although station facilities exist. However trains do stop at all stations early in the morning, late at night and on Sundays. Centre non-platform tracks are provided for Piccadilly line trains at Chiswick Park station; a formation of '1973' stock passes the station with a Cockfosters–Northfields working. *Colin J. Marsden*

Below: The Piccadilly line traverses 40 route miles on an east–west axis, from Cockfosters in the east to Heathrow/Uxbridge in the west. A number of trains terminate short of these destinations, for instance at Arnos Grove at the Cockfosters end, and Rayners Lane on the Uxbridge Line. Departing from the centre siding and approaching Rayners Lane station a train of '1973' stock forms a service bound for Arnos Grove on 20 October 1983. *Colin J. Marsden*

Victoria Line

Walthamstow Central–Brixton
Line type: Tube.
Route miles: 14.
Number of stations served: 16.
   of which, stations with no interchange to other lines: 1 (Pimlico).
Number of trains required to operate service:
   in peak hours, Monday to Friday: 33x8car.
   in off peak, Monday to Friday: 23x8car
   on Saturday: 17x8car.
   on Sunday: 17x8car.
Rolling stock type: '1967' stock.
Main depot: Northumberland Park.
Sidings: Brixton, Victoria and Walthamstow.
Oldest section: Walthamstow Central–Highbury and Islington, opened 1968.
Section in tunnel: All.
Stations with right hand running: King's Cross, Euston and Warren Street.
System records
Only line fully operated by Automatic Train Operation (ATO).
First new tube line to cross central London since 1907.

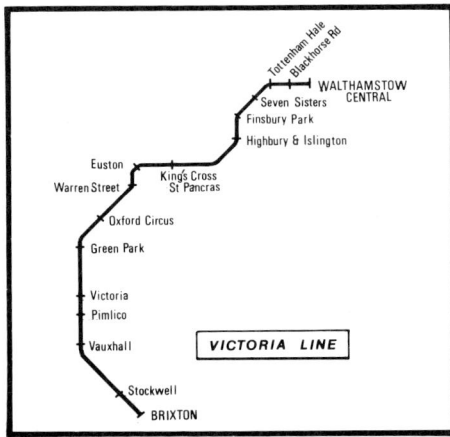

Below: The Victoria line operates a maximum of 33 eight-car trains to provide full passenger services and has depot facilities at Northumberland Park which is served by a non-revenue earning branch from Seven Sisters. A train of stock is seen arriving empty at the depot after forming a passenger service from Brixton on 18 March 1982. *John Glover*

Above: The complete length of the Victoria line is positioned underground, therefore photography is very difficult unless extremely high speed films are used. A northbound train of '1967' stock pulls into Pimlico station during December 1983. Pimlico is the only station on the Victoria line that is not an interchange with another line. *John Glover*

Below: The Victoria line depot at Northumberland Park was opened in 1968 being purpose built for the Victoria line ATO stock and has some 47 sidings. It provides 27 trains for the daily service. This obviously posed view shows sidings 36–47, each with a train of '1967' stock progressively staggered out of the shed. *GEC Traction Ltd*

Stock summary

Type	Line	Number of trains 1984 position	Target position*
Tube			
1938	Bakerloo	15 trains	—
1956	Northern	3 trains	3 trains
1959	Bakerloo	15 trains	30 trains
1959	Northern	60½ trains	46 trains
1960	Central	4 trains	—
1962	Central	84 trains	83½ trains
1962	Northern	2½ trains	4 trains
1967	Victoria	39½ trains	39½ trains
1972 MkI	Northern	30 trains	30 trains
1972 MkII	Jubilee	29 trains	16 trains
1972 MkII	Northern	4 trains	17 trains
1973	Piccadilly	87½ trains	88 trains
1973	Central (ETT)	1 train	1 train
1983	Jubilee	—	15 trains
Surface			
C69/77	District		
C69/77	Metropolitan (H & C/Circle)	139 2-car sets	139 2-car sets
A60/62	Metropolitan (M & EL)	113 4-car sets	113 4-car sets
'D'	District	75 trains	75 trains

* Following full introduction of '1983' stock.

Vehicle types in use on LTE stock

DM	Driving Motor	Vehicle fitted with driver's controls and traction motors.
NDM	Non-Driving Motor	Vehicle fitted with traction/control equipment but *NO* driver's controls or accommodation.
UNDM	Uncoupling Non-Driving Motor	These vehicles are similar to NDM vehicles but have a small control cabinet at one end, allowing uncoupling and shunting of the vehicle/train.
T	Trailer	Trailer Coach not fitted with any driving controls or traction equipment.

Above: This illustration of New Cross Gate station gives a comparison of LTE surface stock and a Southern Region EMU. The LTE train of 'A62' stock has DM No 5129 leading and operating the Metropolitan line East London service, whilst the BR train shows a refurbished 4EPB No 5436 operating a Central Division service bound for London Bridge. *Brian Morrison*

Below: Ruislip Depot played host to the Fellowship of Engineering Exhibition during July 1980 where a number of LTE, BR, and Tyne & Wear Metro vehicles were placed side by side for display purposes. In this view taken on 9 July a 1973 train from the Piccadilly line poses next to a train of 'D' stock. On the right is a match vehicle from the 76 ton diesel-hydraulic crane from BR at Wigan. *Martin Higginson*

A60/62 Stock

Built by: Cravens Ltd

Car types:	DM	T
Length:	53ft 0½in	53ft 0½in
Height:	12ft 1⅛in	12ft 1⅛in
Width:	9ft 8in	9ft 8in
Seating:	54*	58
Weight:	30.80t	21.50t

Numbered from the range:

5000–5123	6000–6123‡
5124–5231†	6124–6231‡

Line: Metropolitan.

Usual train formation: DM(A)　T　T　DM(D)　DM(A)　T　T　DM(D)
　　　　　　　　　　　North　　　　　South　　North　　　　　South

Usual number of trains: 113 four-car sets

* Plus 4 tip-up seats
† Car 5218 fitted with 'D' stock bogies
‡ Fitted with de-icing equipment (some vehicles)

Below: 'A60' stock was ordered from Cravens to coincide with the electrification of the Metropolitan line from Rickmansworth to Amersham and Chesham; the order comprised 124 driving motor and 124 trailer vehicles. Trains are formed of two two-car units thus—DM-T-T-DM—and usually two four-car sets operate together to form eight-car trains. Livery is aluminium with the London Transport legend on the sides DM No 5002 is illustrated. *LTE*

Left: Front end of 'A60/62' stock with route indicator above the centre emergency door. The position of the train number is under the left window with two frontal (white) marker lights below. To the right of these and by the side of the emergency door is a trip cock reset cord, used if the train passes a red signal and the trip cock apparatus is activated. On the buffing beam, blocks are provided each side of a central automatic coupling with air connections below. Red rear and parking lights are also provided. On the left of the buffer beam are two isolating cocks CIC painted yellow used for isolating the coupling face, and UIC painted red, which is the unit isolating cock which, when operated, isolates the complete coupling. Both of these cocks are operated with the driver's reverse handle. Above these and just below the body line is another isolating cock used for isolation of trip cock equipment. On the opposite side of the unit an isolating cock is provided for the drivers safety device. *Colin J. Marsden*

Above: The passenger accommodation in 'A60/62' stock is provided in the 3+2 layout in six bays. Driving cars have two pairs of double leaf, and one single leaf sliding doors. Aluminium roof luggage racks are provided above most seats and route maps are situated over the central gangway walkways. Passenger emergency valves are placed by each exit in the form of a pull down handle. *LTE*

Above: External detail of trailer vehicle No 6048. These vehicles seat 58 passengers and have three sets of double leaf sliding doors on each side, with six opening quarter light windows situated on each side for ventilation. Just above frame height between the two nearest pairs of doors in this illustration, is a small opening with a twist handle, this operates one pair of doors for emergency purposes. *Colin J. Marsden*

Below: External detail of Driving Motor (DM) vehicle, showing only two pairs of double leaf doors with a single door nearest the camera. Again an emergency door control valve is placed just above frame height between the first two doors. At cant rail height between the double leaf doors is the door indicator light which illuminates whenever any door on the coach has not closed correctly. Car No 5137 is illustrated. *Colin J. Marsden*

C69/77 Stock

Built by: Metro-Cammell

Car types:	DM	T
Length:	52ft 7in	49ft 0in
Height:	12ft 1in	12ft 1in
Width:	9ft 7in	9ft 7in
Seating:	32	32
Weight:	31.70t	20.2t

Numbered from the range:

5501–5606	6501–6606*	(C69)
5701–5733	6701–6733	(C77)

Lines: District, Metropolitan (Circle, Hammersmith and City).

Usual train formation:	DM	T	T	DM	T	DM
	DM	T	DM	T	T	DM

Usual number of trains:

District—11 trains.

Metropolitan—35 trains (Circle, Hammersmith and City).

* Some vehicles fitted with de-icing equipment.

Below: The 'C69/77' stock looks very similar to the previously described 'A60/62' types but closer examination will reveal that there are many distinguishing features. The main difference is the four sets of double leaf doors on each car, the omission of side quarter light windows, a large ventilator above the destination indicator, and the most obvious alteration is the provision of two headlights positioned either side of the front door, replacing the previous marker lights. A 'C77' set with DM No 5707 leading approaches Paddington with a Metropolitan line Hammersmith–Whitechapel working on 1 June 1981. *Colin J. Marsden*

Left: Interior of 'C' stock DM which can accommodate 32 passengers. It will be seen that the interior is similar to 'A' stock but low backed seating is arranged in 2+2 transverse arrangement with only one bay between each pair of doors. As the stock was intended for short inner-city trips no roof luggage racks were provided. Route maps were placed above both windows and doors. *LTE*

Above: The outer ends of C stock DM vehicles are fitted with fully automatic couplers with physical, air and electrical connections being made by the units being pushed together. Above the coupler head is a rubbing plate. The isolating cock on the left in the illustration is for the isolation of trip-cock equipment, with a tail light below. On the right side an isolating cock is situated for the driver's safety device, with tail and parking lights below. *John Glover*

D Stock

Built by: Metro-Cammell.

Car types:	DM	UNDM	T
Length:	60ft 3¼in	59ft 5½in	59ft 5½in
Height:	11ft 10½in	11ft 10½in	11ft 10½in
Width:	9ft 4¼in	9ft 4¼in	9ft 4¼in
Seating:	44	48	48
Weight:	27.46t	26.11t	18.40t
Numbered from the range:	7000–7129	8000–8129	17000–17129
	7500–7539*		17500–17538

Line: District.

Usual train formation:	DM(A)	T	UNDM	UNDM	T	DM(D)
	West					East
	DM(A)	T	DM(D)	DM(A)	T	DM(D)
	West		East	West		East

Usual number of trains: 75 trains.

* Fitted with automatic couplers.

Below: The most modern surface type stock is the 'D' type introduced for District line operation from 1979. For the first time a break in LT tradition took place as passenger access was provided by large 3ft 6in wide single leaf doors, with passenger control governed by the guard, whose facilities are provided in the rear driving cab, also fitted with a sliding door. DM No 7500 is illustrated from a three car 'double ended' set. *LTE*

Above: Front end layout of 'D' stock: As it was not intended to have 'in service' coupling/uncoupling, the outer ends of single end units do not have fully automatic couplers; however both ends of double cab units are fitted with fully automatic equipment. Frontal lights are grouped together at buffer beam height and incorporate marker lights, tail lights and 'calling-on' indicator. A trip-cock re-set cable is positioned to the left of the front door in the illustration. A control isolating cock (cut-in/cut-out) rotary switch is situated on the far left. *Colin J. Marsden*

Below: Following serious problems with car ventilation which proved totally inadequate during hot summer weather conditions, an experimental system of ventilation grilles was fitted to DM No 7108 above the side windows. However, this design was not adopted but opening quarter light windows were later introduced and units are currently in the process of being fitted with this modification. DM No 7021 fitted with opening quarter lights is illustrated. *Colin J. Marsden*

Left: Operating on the aft end of single cab units is a Uncoupling Non Driving Motor (UNDM). This is basically the same as a DM but does not have a driving position, only a small control cubicle for uncoupling or shunting. Normal traction equipment is carried on the underframe and the vehicle is mounted on powered bogies. UNDM vehicles are all numbered in the 8xxx range. No 8112 is illustrated at Wimbledon. *Colin J. Marsden*

1938 Stock

Built by: Metro-Cammell/Birmingham RC&W

Car types:	DM	NDM	T
Length:	52ft 3¾in	51ft 2¾in	51ft 2¾in
Height:	9ft 5½in	9ft 5½in	9ft 5½in
Width:	8ft 6$^{1}/_{16}$in	8ft 6$^{1}/_{16}$in	8ft 6$^{1}/_{16}$in
Seating:	42*	40	40
Weight:	27.45t	25.9t	20.67t
Numbered from the range:	10012–10318	120XX range	012160–012414
	11012–11318	121XX range	
		124XX range	

Line: Bakerloo.

Usual train formation:

DM(A)	T	DM(D)	DM(A)	T	NDM	DM(D)
North		South	North			South

Number of units: 16 trains.

* Plus two tip-up seats.

Radios fitted in leading DM(A)(D) cars.

Units scheduled for early withdrawal.

Below: The oldest LT stock still in regular passenger service is the 1938 stock, which now consists of only 16 trains and operates on the Bakerloo line; each train being formed of 7 coaches, ie: DM, T, DM, DM, T, NDM, DM. In this view car 10139 a DM 'A' end north car is seen at Harrow & Wealdstone, the present northern extremity of the line. *John Glover*

Left: Front end detail of 1938 stock DM. To the left of the communicating door the radio aerial can be seen with the 'D' symbol below denoting a D facing car. The train reporting number (200) appears in the centre door, while under the non-drivers window the destination slats can be fitted. The five frontal marker lights are seen on the left front side and below body height two red rear marker lights, coupling isolating and DSD isolating cocks and also the automatic 'Ward' coupling can be found.
John Glover

Below: It is expected that the surviving 1938 stock will be phased out of traffic during early 1985, thus ending an historic chapter in the London Underground story. On 6 June 1984 a 7-car 1938 train departs from Willesden Junction low level with a Harrow & Wealdstone–Elephant train. *Colin J. Marsden*

1956 Stock

Built by: Metro-Cammell/Birmingham RC&W/Gloucester RC&W

Car types:	DM	NDM	T
Length:	52 ft 5$^1/_{16}$in	51ft 2$^{13}/_{16}$in	51ft 2$^{13}/_{16}$in
Height:	9ft 5½in	9ft 5½in	9ft 5½in
Width:	8ft 6¼in	8ft 6¼in	8ft 6¼in
Seating:	42	40	40
Weight:	26.48t	23.61t	20.56t
Numbered from the range:	1000–1011	9000–9009	2000–2010

Line: Northern.

Usual train formation
DM(A)	T	NDM	DM(D)	DM(A)	T	DM(D)
North			South	North		South

Number of sets: 3.

DM(A) North cars fitted with radio equipment.

Below: Three designs of tube train were introduced during 1956 built by Metro-Cammell, Birmingham RC&W and Gloucester RC&W. Each was to serve as a prototype for projected future designs which culminated in the '1959' type stock. Each company produced one train formed of seven cars (DM, T, NDM, DM + DM, T, DM). All were finished in aluminium with blue internal decor. Fluorescent strip lighting was used for the first time, and passenger accommodation was similar to that used on previous types. After introduction the units were put into service on the Piccadilly line but in recent years have operated on the Northern line. The 1956 version can be recognised from the '1959' type by several front differences. The '1956' stock has four front and one tail marker light positioned under the non-driving window, whereas only two can be found on the 1959 stock. The roof also differs considerably, the roof line on the '1956' stock ends at the roof/front edge, whereas the later '1959' type has the roof line on the front under the destination indicator. DM No 1011 leads the Gloucester built train into Charing Cross during December 1983. *John Glover*

1959/62 Stock

Built by: Metro-Cammell, BR Workshops Derby.

Car types:	DM	NDM	T
Length:	52ft 2$\frac{5}{16}$in	51ft 2$\frac{11}{16}$in	51ft 2$\frac{11}{16}$in
Height:	9ft 5½in	9ft 5½in	9ft 5½in
Width:	8ft 6¼in	8ft 6¼in	8ft 6¼in
Seating:	42	40	40
Weight:	26.62t	24.28t	20.67t
Numbered from the range:			
	1012–1315	9205–9225	2202–2224*
	1612–1751†	9013–9313	2012–2314*
		9613–9749†	2612–2750*†

Lines: Bakerloo, Northern, Central.

Usual train formation:

Bakerloo	DM(A)	T	NDM	DM(D)	DM(A)	T	DM(D)
(1959 stock)	North			South	North		South
Northern	DM(A)	T	NDM	DM(D)	DM(A)	T	DM(D)
(1959 stock)	North			South	North		South
Central	DM(A)	T	NDM	DM(D)	DM(A)	T	DM(D)
(1962 stock)	West			East	West		East

Usual number of trains:

Bakerloo—15 trains.

Northern—63 trains.

Central—84 trains.

Northern Line DM(A) vehicles fitted with radio equipment.

† Including half train of 1962 stock.

* Some trailers fitted with de-icing equipment.

Below: View inside Ruislip depot showing a number of 1959/62' type units receiving repairs. The deep pits between the tracks are provided to enable men to walk at full height the complete length under a unit for inspection. For staff safety, no electric rails are provided in depots, power being taken to the unit by trolley wires visibly plugged into the unit behind the man on the stool in the illustration. When receiving attention units carry a red disc on the front informing other staff that the unit is being worked on. *LTE*

Left: After successful trials with '1956' tube stock orders were placed with Metro-Cammell for 76 seven-car units to replace a number of pre-1938 trains. Cars of three types were introduced Driving Motors (DM), Trailers (T), and Non Driving Motors (NDM). Soon after the first order was placed a further batch was ordered from Birmingham RC&W and BR. However Birmingham RC&W were unable to undertake their build and Metro-Cammell were awarded the contract for 338 DM and 112 NDM vehicles; the BR contract was for 169 Trailers. Metro-Cammell DM 'D' end south middle No 1037 is illustrated at Neasden. *John Glover*

Right: External detail of 1959 DM No 1266, an A end North middle vehicle. The orange door indicator light can be seen on the roof, and just above sole bar height an emergency door control handle is situated. Internal seating in DM vehicles is for 42 arranged in 2+2 transverse in the middle and in longitudinal pattern at car ends. *John Glover*

47

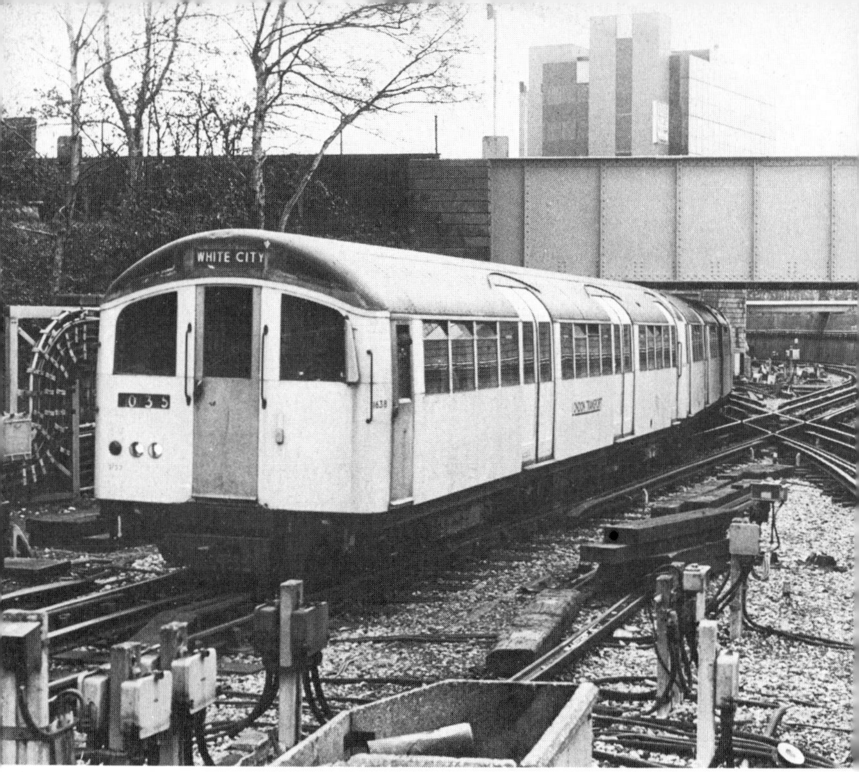

Above: Until recent years, no detail differences existed between 1959 and 1962 vehicles. However, the red stabling lights now fitted are to the left of the marker lights on 1962 stock, but to the right on 1959 stock. Location can, of course, assist in identification as '1959' stock is normally allocated to the Northern/Bakerloo lines whilst 1962 stock is used on the Central line. A train of 1962 stock led by DM No 1638 shunts at White City prior to operating a service to Liverpool Street on 6 February 1980. *John Glover*

Left: Front end detail of '1962' stock (also applicable to 1959 vehicles). The destination indicator is at the top controlled by a manual handle on the inside. The train number is carried under the non driving window with two front and one rear marker light below. The four buffer beam cocks are from left to right: trip cock isolating, unit isolating, coupling isolating and driver's safety device. Red marker lights are also on the buffer beam. An automatic coupling is in the centre with rubbing plate above. *Colin J. Marsden*

Above: '1962' stock Trailer, showing two double leaf and two single leaf doors; these vehicles accommodate 40 passengers with room for up to another 50 standing. The door indicator light can be seen on the roof just above cant rail height and the door close button on the end. This vehicle is fitted with de-icing equipment. Identified by the letter 'D' under the number, it is mounted on a special beam at the far end. *Colin J. Marsden*

Below: '1962' stock driving motor vehicles have only two double and one single leaf door on each side, the driving door being of the hinged type openable by using the reverser key. 1962 stock is used almost entirely on the Central line and formed into four-car sets. DM 'A' West No 1412 is illustrated coupled in the middle of an eight-car formation. *Colin J. Marsden*

1960 Stock

Built by: Cravens Ltd (DM vehicles only).

Car types:	DM	T‡
Length:	52ft 0⅜in	51ft 2¾in
Height:	9ft 5½in	9ft 5½in
Width:	8ft 6¼in	8ft 6⁷/₁₆in
Seating:	40	40
Weight:	29.89t	20.67t

Numbered from the range:

3900–3911   4921–4927*

(some numbers not issued)

Line: Central.

Usual train formation: DM(A)   T   DM(D)
West   East

Number of units: 3†.

* Fitted with de-icing equipment.

† Three units remain in service out of six originally formed, plus four spare cars.

‡ Refurbished 1938 stock trailers.

Above: During 1960 12 experimental DM cars were ordered from Cravens Ltd for use on the Central line to gauge passenger reaction and technical performance, prior to production sets being ordered. Trailer vehicles were needed to operate between these motor cars and these were provided by converting 12 pre-1938 trailers and forming six four-car units (DM, T, T, DM). One of the main difference between these and the previously described types is the provision of two large windows between the door openings on DMs in place of the four small hereto used. DM No 3900 is illustrated. *GEC Traction Ltd*

Above: From 1964 five of the six units were converted for automatic train operation (ATO) tests and during modification the cab side doors were sealed up and a drop light window fitted. On the front end the train number plates were repositioned on the central door and the trip cock reset cord also repositioned on the front enabling the train operator to reset the device without leaving the cab. A train of '1960' stock led by car No 3904 arrives at Roding Valley with a Woodford–Hainault train on 23 February 1979. *John Glover*

Below: From 1976 a start was made on replacing the two pre-1938 trailer cars in each set with one converted 1938 trailer. Replacement of all vehicles was planned but prohibitive costs prevented this and eventually only two units were so treated receiving one new trailer each, making three-car units. A three-car formation with DM No 3908 nearest the camera, departs from Roding Valley with a Woodford train on 18 March 1982. *John Glover*

Note:
It should be noted that until 1983 two four-car units remained in service based at Hainault incorporating pre-1938 trailers; these have now been withdrawn, the DM cars being stored and the trailers scrapped.

1967 Stock

Built by: Metro-Cammell.

Car types:	DM	T
Length:	52ft 9½in	52ft 9½in
Height:	9ft 5$\frac{1}{64}$in	9ft 5$\frac{1}{16}$in
Width:	8ft 8in	8ft 8in
Seating:	40	36
Weight:	28.50t	19.40t

Numbered from the range:

	3001–3079	4001–4079
	3101–3179	4101–4179

Line: Victoria.

Usual train formation:

Victoria: DM(A)   T   T   DM(D)   DM(A)   T   T   DM(D)
           North   South   North   South

Usual number of trains: 39½ trains.
All fitted for ATO.

Above: Following successful trials with the 1960 ATO trains on the Woodford–Hainault line a decision was made to operate the new Victoria line with automatic control stock. For this service Metro-Cammell built a total of 79 four-car units formed DM, T, T, DM. This stock resembled the '1960' sets in many ways retaining the two long windows between door positions. The cab ends incorporated a number of revisions including wrap round windows to improve visibility, two high-powered headlights and a 'calling on' light above the driver's side window. DM No 3179 is illustrated. *John Glover*

Above: Interior of Victoria line stock. The interiors of DM and T vehicles of the 1967 build differ with DM cars having longitudinal seating at the car ends and two bays of transverse seats 2+2 in the middle, providing seats for 40 passengers. On Trailer vehicles all seating is longitudinal thus reducing seating accommodation to 36. One innovation on the '1967' stock was the extension of door window height to improve visibility for standing passengers. The interior of DM No 3177 is shown. *John Glover*

Below: For the first time on an LTE train the driving cab had only one control handle for power and braking, although this is not frequently used as when in normal service trains travel under the ATO mode. When required for manual operation a flag switch is operated on the non-driving side and speed is restricted to 10mph. Fault and failure diagnostic equipment is positioned in the cab. Six 1967 units are seen at Northumberland Park depot. *LTE*

1972 Stock (MkI and MkII)

Built by: Metro-Cammell.

Car types:	DM	UNDM	T
Length:	52ft 9½in	52ft 5in	52ft 5in
Height:	9ft 5¹/₆₄in	9ft 5¹/₆₄in	9ft 5¹/₆₄in
Width:	8ft 8in	8ft 8in	8ft 8in
Seating:	40	40	36
Weight:			
MkI	28.2t	26.8t	18.6t
MkII	27.8t	26.5t	18.1t
Numbered from the range:			
MkI	3201–3230	4201–4230	3401–3430
	3301–3330	4301–4330	
	3501–3530*	4501–4530	
MkII	3231–3263	4231–4263	3431–3463
	3331–3363	4331–4363	
	3531–3563*	4531–4563	

Lines: Jubilee, Northern.

Usual train formation:	DM(A)	T	T	DM(D)	UNDM(A)	T	M(D)
	North			South	End Middle		South

Usual number of trains:
Jubilee Line—29 trains (MkII stock).
Northern Line—30 trains (MkI stock).
Northern Line—4 trains (MkII stock).
* Fitted with mechanical couplers.
A end North leading/D end South leading, DMs fitted with radio equipment.

Below: Two distinct batches of '1972' stock are in service—Mk I and Mk II. External appearance of the vehicles closely resembles the 1967 type but recognition factors do exist. '1972' Mk I stock is formed into three and four-car sets operating in trains as 7 car formations and allocated to the Northern line. Recognition between these and 1967 stock can be gained by the following—no 'calling on' lights, and additional isolating cocks at buffing level. 1972 Mk I DM No 3526 of a three-car unit is illustrated.
John Glover

Above: The four-car units are formed DM, T, T, DM and have fully automatic couplers at both ends. Three-car units are formed DM, T, UNDM and have automatic couplers on the UNDM but only mechanical couplers on the DM cars, as these are not normally required for 'active' coupling. UNDM vehicles carry control equipment recovered from redundant 1938/49 stock. DM 'A' No 3227 from a four-car set fitted with automatic couplers, arrives at Finchley Central on 15 March 1983 with a southbound train for Morden via Bank. *John Glover*

Above: Following the initial order for 90 DM, 90 Trailers and 30 UNDM vehicles, a further build of 99 DM, 99 Trailers and 33 UNDM vehicles was authorised, these becoming '1972' Mk II vehicles. Several detail differences exist on these vehicles from the Mk I build the main being: fitting of 'calling on' lights, repositioned train number plates from the central door to the non-driving window, painting of passenger doors red and the replacement of the Underground insignia with a roundel. A train of 1972 Mk II stock stops at Canons Park during 1982. When introduced Mk I and Mk II vehicles were not compatible, but modifications are now being made to enable inter-coupling. *John Glover*

Above: At the current time '1972' Mk II stock is used on the Jubilee line except for one train on the Northern. Formations are identical to 1972 Mk I sets. DM 'D' end South Middle No 3342 is illustrated, coupled to UNDM 'A' middle No 3442. The seating in DM cars is for 40 passengers in both longitudinal and transverse configuration. *Colin J. Marsden*

Below: '1972' Mk II Trailer vehicle with red livery doors and roundel. The seating capacity of the trailers is 36 and the vehicles weigh 18.1 tons in operational condition. Slit openings above the windows are ventilators controllable from the inside. The door indicator light is positioned on the roof at the near end, with the emergency door control valve above sole bar height at the far end. Trailer No 4262 is shown. *Colin J. Marsden*

1973 Stock

Built by: Metro-Cammell.

Car types:	DM	UNDM	T
Length:	57ft 3¾in	57ft 1½in	57ft 1½in
Height:	9ft 5⁷/₆₄in	9ft 5⁷/₆₄in	9ft 5⁷/₆₄in
Width:	8ft 7½in	8ft 7½in	8ft 7½in
Seating:	44	44	44
Weight:	27.20t	26.20t	18.40t
Numbered from the range:	100–253 854–895*	300–453	500–594

Lines: Piccadilly, Central (ETT set).

Usual train formation: DM   T   UNDM   UNDM   T   DM
                             DM   T   DM (double cab units)

Usual number of trains: 87½ trains—Piccadilly.
                            1 train (3 car)—Central ETT set.

* Fitted with automatic couplers.

Below: '1973' tube stock was constructed for service on the Piccadilly line and commenced operation from mid 1975. The units are similar to the previous '1972' type but a number of modifications are incorporated. Recognition of the type is made easy as the ends have the lower half painted red. The first 16 units have black roofs and are thus identifiable from the remainder of the fleet. A later set arrives at Rayners Lane with a train from Arnos Grove on 17 March 1983. *John Glover*

Top: The front end of '1973' stock is very similar to '1972' Mk II cars, except that the train number position has again been moved and is now incorporated in the body under the non-driving window. To the right of the number in the same panel is a Maltese cross which when showing indicates that weak field has been selected. The majority of 1973 vehicles are formed into three car units DM, T, UNDM, and of these, DM cars have mechanical couplers fitted and UNDM have fully automatic couplers. However there are 19 double cab units formed DM, T, DM and these have fully automatic couplers on both DM vehicles. This view at Acton Town shows DM No 885 on the left with an automatic coupler, and DM No 165 with mechanical coupler on the right. *Colin J. Marsden*

Above: 1973 Trailer vehicles are very similar to the '1972' type but are considerably longer—57ft 1½in—compared to 52ft 5in, the additional space taken up by longer windows and luggage area at the vehicle ends. 1973 Trailer No 550 is illustrated. Door close button, door indicator light and emergency door valves are all visible. *Colin J. Marsden*

Above: 154 UNDM vehicles are in service numbered 300–453. These are basically the same as DM vehicles except that no driving position is provided, control of the motors and automatic coupling equipment being housed in a small cupboard at the outer end. Vehicles weigh 26.2 tons and seat 44 passengers. No 337 is illustrated. *Colin J. Marsden*

Below: With the design of new underground stock in mind the final two double cab sets of '1973' stock were delivered as prototype/test units, fitted with thyristor 'chopper' control equipment, one having a Westinghouse and the other GEC designed systems. The two units were entitled Experimental Tube Trains—ETT for short. The Westinghouse unit was delivered during 1977 and operated first on the Acton Town–Northfields section and later on the Woodford–Hainault line. The GEC unit was delivered in 1979 and commenced running tests in 1980. From late 1983 the Westinghouse set commenced passenger operation on the Woodford–Hainault line. The two driving motor cars have been extensively rebuilt with the saloon cab side of the first set of doors blocked off. External appearance is basically the same as conventional 1973 stock except for a trip-cock wire positioned outside the front door for ease of access and an additional windowscreen wiper fitted on the non-driving window. ETT set formed 893, 692, 892 stands at Hainault on 30 January 1984. The GEC unit is likely to be rebuilt to standard form in the near future. *Colin J. Marsden*

1983 Stock

Built by: Metro-Cammell.

Car types:	DM	T
Length:	56ft 6½in	57ft 10in
Height:	9ft 5⅛in	9ft 5⅛in
Width:	8ft 7¼in	8ft 7¼in
Seating:	48	48
Weight:	27.76t	20.73t

Numbered from the range:
3601–3630   4601–4630
3701–3730

Line: Jubilee.

Usual train formation:

DM(A)	T	DM(D)	DM(A)	T	DM(D)
North		South	North		South

Usual number of trains: 15 trains.

Above: General view of '1983' stock, showing two three-car units coupled together. The first units were delivered at the end of 1983 and commenced trial and test running from Neasden depot shortly afterwards. DM No 3604 is leading in this picture. *Colin J. Marsden*

Left: Front end layout of '1983' tube stock. It will be noticed that larger front windows have been fitted to this stock. Above the shatter proof glass driving window a radio aerial can be seen, with fully automatic couplers in the centre of the buffing beam with headlight, tail light and parking lights, either side. Train reporting numbers are carried under the non-driving window.
Colin J. Marsden

Below: '1983' stock trailer car. It will be noticed that four single leaf sliding doors passenger controlled are fitted on trailer vehicles. The 'door open' warning lights are on the sloping section of the roof whilst the emergency door valve is positioned on the body side at the far end. Trailer vehicles seat 48 passengers. *Colin J. Marsden*

1986 Prototype/1990 Tube stock

Design work is now well under way on the replacement stock for the large fleet of 1959/62 cars, which together operate services on the Bakerloo and Central, and form much of the Northern Line fleet. Priority is to be given to the Central Line, and three 4-car prototypes are being constructed, to be ready in 1986. Fleet orders will be placed in 1987, with a view to delivery from 1990 onwards. The final decision on specifications will be a compromise based on capital and maintenance costs, commercial and technical requirements, and political considerations.

A standardised rolling stock design for all lines gives the opportunity to move vehicles freely around the system as requirements change over the years, and allows a general flexibility of policy. However, the lines are all physically different. Thus Central Line curvature, particularly at Bank, will not allow the use of six longer cars to replace the present eight. For engineering as well as operating reasons it is desirable to use symmetrical trains wherever possible, and seven cars bring more problems than they solve . Short platform lengths on the Northern Line at around 330ft mean that six standard length cars will only occupy 310ft, resulting in wasted capacity. With the fall in passenger traffic though, this may not matter. For the Central Line, eight-car trains of about the present car length, consisting of four identical two-car units are to be used.

Metro-Cammell will build two of the four-car prototypes and the third will come from British Rail Engineering Ltd at Derby. Electrical equipment for one of the trains to be built by Metro-Cammell will be supplied by GEC-TPL of Manchester, and for the second by Brown Boveri of Zurich. Brush Electrical Machines Ltd will provide the equipment for the BREL train.

Each of the three prototypes will consist of two two-car units, with one car having a driving cab and the other no cab; they will be about 16m and 15.6m long respectively, and will be semi-permanently coupled as a pair. The automatic coupling arrangements between units and the controls of all three trains are designed to be compatible so that any combination of two-car units can couple to form an eight-car train for service trials. This will increase flexibility during the trial period and enable an eight-car train to be tried in public service while engineers are making tests on the remaining cars.

The main technical features to be tested on the prototypes are:
* Welded aluminium alloy bodies, including the floor structure.
* External sliding doors.
* Air suspension.
* Dimpled rubber-type floors.
* All axles motored with chopper control.
* Lightweight fully sprung motors, with flexible drives to axle mounted gearboxes (Metro-Cammell trains).
* A new design of steerable bogie. These bogies will have the more usual axle-mounted motors, but with disc brakes on the motor shafts (BREL trains).
* Smaller wheels which hardly protrude above floor level.
* Improved ventilation and more effective heating with thermostatic control.

Dot matrix train destination indicators on the train front will be linked to similar indicators inside each end of every car. The interior indicators will normally show the destination but, as the train approaches each station, trackside 'trigger' equipment will change the display to name the next station and an audible signal will sound.

Passenger facilities will include door-opening buttons (mounted on the doors), and internal door closing buttons for use at terminals. There will be special tones to indicate when doors may be opened or are about to close.

Three internal layouts are to be tried out, with substantially increased standing space by comparison with present tube stock. The main aisle down the car centres is to be as wide as possible to provide more standing space, and the number of seats per car will vary from 32 to 42 per car, depending on layout.

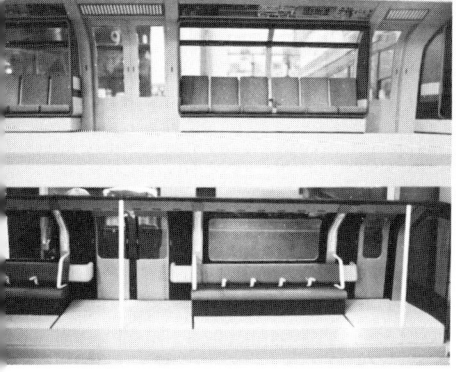

Left: Internal mock-up of two design alternatives for '1990' generation tube stock. The upper model has individual seats with no armrests whilst the lower is of more conventional design. It is interesting to note that double leaf doors are included on both mock-ups.
John Glover

Service Stock

Electric Locomotives

Number	Use	Former identity	Builder	Year built
L11	Shunter (Acton)	DMs 3080/3109	Metro-Cammell	1931
L2 *Sarah Siddons*	Test Loco	Metropolitan Loco No 12	Metropolitan–Vickers	1922
L13A/B	Shunter (Acton)	DMs 10130/11130	Metro-Cammell	1938

Above: The London Transport works at Acton has the need for a tractor unit to enable free movement of stock around the works complex. For this purpose electric locomotive No L11 was introduced in 1964 converted from two pre-1938 motor cars Nos 3080/3109 of 1931 vintage. The locomotive has powered bogies at both ends and is painted in yellow livery. The machine always operates facing the same way and different coupling facilities are provided at either end. This view of the 'A' end (facing Acton Town) is fitted with tube couplers and nose end air pipes. *John Glover*

Top: The business or 'D' end of locomotive No L11 is more interesting as it carries two couplings one at compatible height for tube sized vehicles, and the other at surface stock height. A coupling observation window is fitted in the centre door and a downward facing floodlight is fixed at roof height. Again waist height air connections are provided. Trip-cock and DSD isolating cocks are on the buffing beam. *John Glover*

Above: Probably the most famous LT electric locomotive is No 12 *Sarah Siddons*, one of 20 Metropolitan Vickers built machines introduced in 1922/23 for use on the Metropolitan line. After passenger services were taken over by unit stock, four locomotives were transferred to the service department; two machines were eventually cut up, one was placed on display in the LT Museum and the fourth No 12 was retained as a brake block test locomotive. It was restored and exhibited at the BR Rail 150 Exhibition at Shildon in 1975 and now carries this embellishment under its nameplate. *John Glove.*

Above: During May 1982 No 12 passed through Acton works for a classified overhaul and emerged painted in early LPTB livery with gold lining and red window surrounds. The locomotive was used on some enthusiast specials later in the year, hauling BR stock over the Metropolitan lines. Following this enthusiasm for the machine grew considerably and it was displayed at BR Open Days at Eastleigh, Brighton and Stratford during 1983. On 26 May 1983 No 12 worked under its own power on the Southern Region prior to operating to Eastleigh and is captured on film here passing Wimbledon West on a test working from Wimbledon Park to Strawberry Hill depot.
Colin J. Marsden

Left: Front end of No 12 *Sarah Siddons*. On the front end there are three marker lights with a central route indicator position and above buffer beam height on the right is a train reporting number position. Waist level main reservoir and brake pipes are also situated here and duplicated on the buffer beam. Conventional draw gear is provided on the beam with a large control fuse underneath. Note the wing mirror on the driver's (right) side.
John Glover

Top: A number of specials featuring No 12 have been operated on BR tracks and these cause considerable organisation as the locomotive needs to be worked by LT staff with relevant BR conductors. No 12 was photographed hauling the SR green 4SUB unit No 4732 past Woking Junction while returning from Eastleigh Open Day. *Colin J. Marsden*

Above: A rather interesting power twin, classified as a locomotive, operates as a works shunter at Acton Works and is numbered L13A and L13B. It was introduced in 1974 by coupling two 1938 stock PMs together and fitted with high level air pipes. It was painted red when first used but has subsequently been outshopped in service maroon. The locomotive is usually used to shift stock across gaps in the live rail. *LURS Society*

Battery Locomotives

Number range	Built by	Year built
L15–L16	Metro-Cammell	1970
L17–L19	Metro-Cammell	1971
L20–L21	Metro-Cammell	1964
L22–L32	Metro-Cammell	1965
L33	LT Acton	1962 (formerly L76 until 1974)
L35–L40	Gloucester RC&W	1938
L44–L54	BREL Doncaster	1974
L55–L60	Pickering	1951
L61	Pickering	1952
L61–L67	Metro-Cammell	1985 (under construction)

Below: The LT battery locomotives are fitted with driving positions at both ends and constructed to tube size gauge. Although classified as battery locomotives these machines can operate direct from the live rail supply if available but usually use their battery power as their normal operation is when electric power is switched off. No L18 hauls an engineers train formed of flat wagons and personnel carriers out of Lillie Bridge during August 1978. *John Glover*

Above: Various batches of battery locomotives have been constructed. Machines numbered L20–L32 were built by Metro-Cammell during 1964 and when introduced were in maroon livery but in recent years a number have been outshopped in service yellow, as displayed here on No L21. This machine is fitted with buck-eye couplers at one end, other buffer beam equipment consists of main reservoir/brake pipes, control jumper receptacles and trip-cock, drivers safety device isolating cocks. *John Glover*

Below: Normally the LT workshops at Acton can undertake all repairs to their equipment, however during August 1982 loco No L26 was taken to BREL Doncaster works for fractured frame repairs and was photographed on works jacks during October. All buffers on battery locomotives are hinged enabling them to be raised clear for coupling to passenger stock. *Ray Anthony*

Above: Front end detail of battery locomotive No L33 with buffers in the raised or stored position. Conventional shackle draw gear can be seen on the buffer beam with Ward type couplings below. In addition to air connections, control jumper cable sockets are also provided. No L33 was constructed by LT at Acton Works in 1962. *John Glover*

Above: All battery locomotives constructed post 1964 carry two air compressors enabling single operation if required, although is it unusual practice. When delivered all battery locomotives were in maroon service livery but from Spring 1979 locomotives that had received shopping emerged in yellow. In its latest guise, but looking rather the worse for wear, No L32, built in 1965, stands inside Neasden depot during April 1983. *John Glover*

Below: To supplement the fleet of battery locomotives a further fleet of 11 were constructed during 1973 by BREL Doncaster works, of the same basic design with grilles running the full length on one side, and in four panels at both ends on the other. Doncaster built No L46 shunts service stock at Lillie Bridge depot on 27 July 1983. *Ian Cowley*

Note:
A further order has been placed for six new locomotives fitted with new type couplers, retractable buffers and a revised method of battery removal.

Diesel Locomotives

Number	Tender No	Works No*	Builder	Year built
DL81	DT81	10278	Rolls Royce	1968
DL82	DT82	10272	Rolls Royce	1968
DL83	DT83	10271	Rolls Royce	1967
L84 (A456NWX)	—	Type U1000	Mercedes-Benz Unimog	1983

* Number applicable to loco only.

Above: From 1971 LT acquired three secondhand Sentinel diesel-hydraulic 0-6-0 shunters to replace their last steam locomotives. The diesels were built in 1967/8 by Rolls Royce of Shrewsbury and had been previously owned by Thomas Hill of Rotherham. These machines are painted in green livery and operate at Neasden and Lillie Bridge on depot shunting duties; they are not permitted to operate on the main line. No DL82 is illustrated. *John Glover*

Above: A bogie tender is permanently coupled to these locomotives at the cab end which carries no conventional buffing gear. These are built onto the bogies of withdrawn Q stock and required to operate track circuit equipment as the locomotives will not do so on their own. The upper illustration shows the tender to No DL81, numbered DT81. No through brake connections are provided, but both shackle and Ward type couplers are fitted. The lower illustration shows locomotive No DL81. it will be noticed that fixed buffers are carried and couplings of both the shackle and ward type are also fitted. *Both: John Glover*

Above and left: The latest addition to the LT locomotive fleet is the Unimog shunter numbered L84. This vehicle is a road/rail unit and used for shunting operations, normally at Ealing Common. The Unimog painted in service yellow livery is licenced for public road use and carries the licence plate A 456 NWX. End connections are compatible for shunting service stock, air pipes being fitted on the nose end. The upper illustration shows No L84 soon after delivery in its road mode, while the lower view shows the vehicle during April 1984 in its rail entity.
Both: R. J. Greenaway

Electric Sleet Locomotives

Number	Built†	Introduced‡	Builder	Original Nos§	Location (1984)
ESL107	1903	1939	Metro/Birmingham	3944/81	Acton
ESL117*	1903	1940	Metro/Birmingham	3954/95	Stonebridge
ESL118A/B*	1932	1961	Birmingham	2758/49	Neasden

* Withdrawn and awaiting disposal.
† Date of original construction.
‡ Date introduced as sleet locomotive.
§ Central London Railway/LPTB Number.

Below: The need to keep electrified rails clear of ice or snow caused conversion during 1939/40 of 18 tube sized electric sleet locomotives (ESLs). Each locomotive was formed of two 1903 ex-Central London Railway DM vehicles welded together to form one vehicle. The de-icing equipment was carried on two centre unpowered bogies whilst the outer bogies retained the traction equipment. The ESLs have a driving position at each end and a tank for the de-icing fluid is in the centre, with large access doors adjacent to the tank on each side. Of the 18 ESLs converted only one still remains in service in early 1985. No ESL107, allocated to Acton Works, is illustrated here in yellow livery. *John Glover*

Right: De-icing and sleet equipment as carried on ESL stock. On the left is the de-icing fluid layer controlled from the operating panel inside the vehicle. In the centre of the de-icing beam are two sleet brushes flanking an ice breaking wheel. *LTE*

Below right: Following the electrification of the Metropolitan line beyond Rickmansworth during 1961, a further de-icing set was required. A two-car unit was built formed of redundant 'T' stock vehicles, semi-permanently coupled back to back and numbered ESL118A and ESL118B. During 1980 the unit entered Acton Works and was modified for leaf cleaning duties between Rickmansworth and Amersham; for this application flat wagon No F311 was coupled between the cars and carried additional equipment. Viewed from the 'A' end the de-icing unit and leaf cleaning train is seen at Acton Works during July 1983. *John Glover*

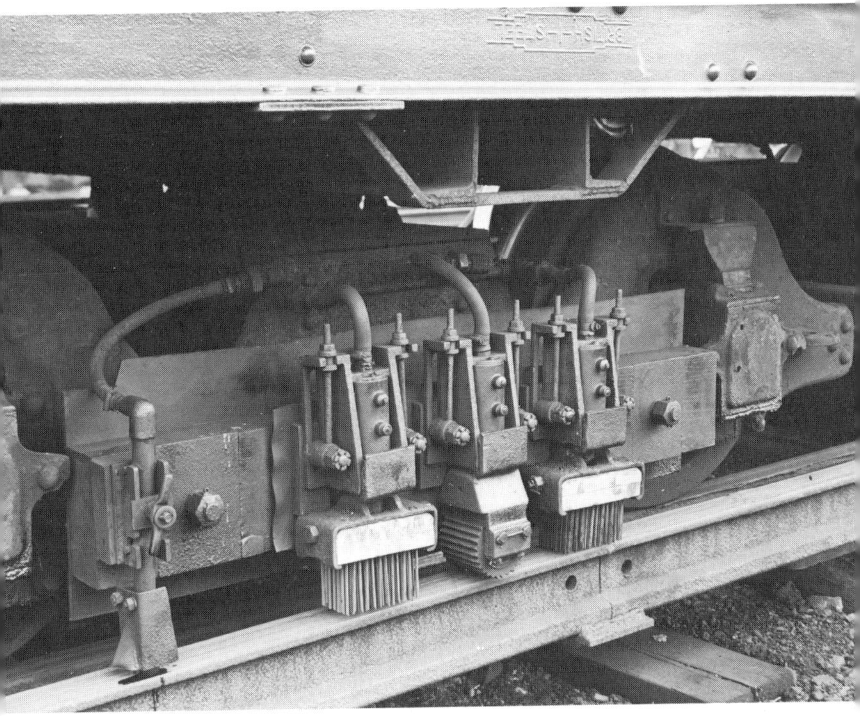

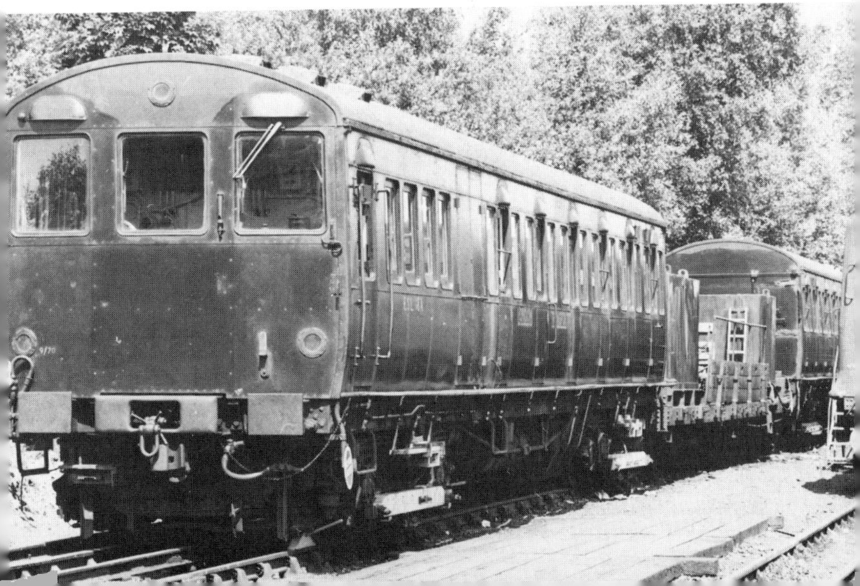

Pilot Motors

Surface

Number range	Year built	Former identity	Year converted
L126–L127	1938	Q Stock 4416, 4417	1971

Tube

Number range	Year built	Former identity	Year converted
L130–L131	1934	Pre 38 stock 3690/93	1967
L134	1927	Pre 38 stock 3370	1967
L135	1934	Pre 38 stock 3701	1967

Below: For movement of non-service stock around the system and in particular between depots, a small number of pilot motor cars exist. For transporting surface stock two former Q38 DMs, Nos 4116/17, are used, and numbered L127 and L128. The pair are painted in yellow livery and are usually kept at Ruislip where they have been used to shunt stock in recent years. *John Glover*

Above: Eight pre-1938 stock DMs were transferred to the service department early in 1967 to act as tube size pilot motors; after a considerable period of time at Acton works four were actually converted and the others went for scrap. Cars are usually kept in pairs and act as match/escort cars for tube vehicles when required for movement, one car being placed at either end of the train. The upper illustration shows cars L130/131 which were converted from DMs Nos 3690/3693. Livery is yellow and the LT insignia is in red. The lower plate shows pilot motors Nos L134/135 which were rebuilt from DMs 3370/3701. End connections are of the standard pattern on both pairs and Ward type couplers are fitted.
Both: John Glover

Ballast Motor Cars

Number	Year built	Built by	Converted	Former identity
L140	1938	Metro-Cammell	1980	10182
L141	1938	Metro-Cammell	1973	11067
L142	1938	Metro-Cammell	1973	10021
L143	1938	Metro-Cammell	1973	10065
L144	1938	Metro-Cammell	1975	10257
L145	1938	Metro-Cammell	1975	11027
L146	1938	Metro-Cammell	1976	10034
L147	1938	Metro-Cammell	1976	11034
L148	1938	Metro-Cammell	1977	11022
L149	1938	Metro-Cammell	1977	11104
L150*	1938	Metro-Cammell	1978	10327
L151*	1938	Metro-Cammell	1978	11327
L152	1938	Metro-Cammell	1978	10266
L153	1938	Metro-Cammell	1978	11266
L154	1938	Metro-Cammell	1978	10141
L155	1938	Metro-Cammell	1978	11141

* Reserved for weed killing train operation.

Below: Sixteen ballast motor cars are in operation and used in connection with engineering workings. All are rebuilds of 1938 DM vehicles but many modifications have been made including the fitting of nose end air pipes, air operated warning horns and revised internal layout. Two unidentified motors are seen here painted in maroon livery. *LURS collection*

Above: Ballast motors which are numbered in the locomotive 'L' series were all painted in maroon livery when converted, however several now carry engineering department yellow livery as displayed here on No L144, converted from DM No 10257 in 1975. *LURS collection*

Below: Two of the ballast motor cars Nos L150/151 converted from DM Nos 10327 and 11327 are used on the weed control train. Spraying weed killer from the front of the cars just below the centre door, the tanks and chemical are stored in the former seating position. The cars are easily recognisable from others of the same type by the yellow/black warning panel on the nose door. The train was photographed in operation near Rickmansworth. *LURS collection*

Miscellaneous Departmental Vehicles

Four wheel flat wagons

Number Range	Load	Built by	Year built
F305	10 tonnes	Shildon	1944
F328–F329	10 tonnes	Gloucester RC&W	1935

Bogie flat wagons

Number Range	Load	Built by	Year built
F311–F315	30 tonnes	Metro-Cammell	1931
F316–F322	30 tonnes	Gloucester	1935
F331–F340	30 tonnes	Gloucester	1937
F341–F371*	30 tonnes	Gloucester	1951
F372–F375	30 tonnes	Gloucester	1956
F377	30 tonnes	LT Acton Works	1959
F380–F383	30 tonnes	Gloucester	1959
F384–F391	30 tonnes	BR Ashford	1965
F392–F398	30 tonnes	BR Ashford	1966

Several vehicles of type withdrawn from stock.
* Some vehicles fitted with mobile cement mixers.

Notes
F311 fitted with water tank.
F340 fitted with Smalley 3009 concrete breaker.
F341 fitted with tank for drain emptying.
F342/3/5/50/1/5 fitted with concrete mixers.
F352 fitted with Steiner HSM800 Trench digger.
F356 fitted with large bin for rubbish collection.

Four-wheel hopper wagons

Number Range	Load	Built by	Year built
HW403–HW406	20 tonnes	Gloucester	1935
HW415–HW428	20 tonnes	Gloucester	1951
HW435–HW437	20 tonnes	BR Shildon	1965

Several vehicles of type withdrawn from stock.

Bogie hopper wagons

Number Range	Load	Built by	Year built
HW201–HW222	30 tonnes	W H Davis	1981

Rail wagons

Number Range	Load	Built by	Year built
RW454–RW458	20 tonnes	Metro-Cammell	1931
RW460–RW464	20 tonnes	Gloucester	1935
RW466–RW475	20 tonnes	Gloucester	1937
RW476–RW487	20 tonnes	Gloucester	1950
RW488–RW494	20 tonnes	Gloucester	1958
RW495–RW506	20 tonnes	BR Ashford	1965

some vehicles of type withdrawn from stock.

Notes:
RW469 has no bogies—works mounted on top of RW465.
RW490 fitted with electric hoist for long rail trains.
RW490–504 fitted with 'hoop' siderails for operation with five car long rail trains.

General purpose wagons

Number Range	Weight	Built by	Year built
GP901–GP941	30 tonnes	Procor	1984

Brake vans

Number Range	Weight	Built by	Year built
B556–B560	20 tonnes	Hurst Nelson	1935
B580–B585*	20 tonnes	BR Ashford	1965

Some vehicles of type withdrawn from stock.

Notes:
*B580/585 used as tube stock match vehicles.
B582/583 also carry numbers LTE 95800, LTE 95801 for identification on BR TOPS
wagon system.
B583/584 used as surface stock match vehicles.

Bogie well wagon

Number	Year built	Formerly
WPW 1000	1937	Diesel generator wagon until 1975

Cable drum wagons

Number Range	Built by	Year built
CW1050–CW1052	Gloucester	1940

Gauging car

G663   Converted from pre-1938 trailer 7131 of 1931 vintage in 1963—tube size vehicle.

Rail grinding cars

RG 802   Converted from pre-1938 control trailer 5241 in 1956.
RG 803   Converted from pre-1938 control trailer 5245 in 1956.

Personnel carriers

PC850–PC859   Converted from pre-1938, and 1938 stock between 1965–1981. Some vehicles of type now withdrawn.

Tunnel cleaning train

TCC1–TCC5   Special train introduced 1972–1977 formed of 1938 stock DM's 10226, 10087 with three special cleaning cars between.

Track recording trailer

TRC 912   Converted 1978 from 1938 trailer 012331.

Permanent way cranes—diesel-electric

Number	Built by	Year built
C606	Ransome & Rapier	1931
DEC 617–618	Taylor Hubbard	1955–1956
DEC 622	Taylor Hubbard	1964
C623	Cowans Sheldon	1982

Jib carriers

Number	Year built	Additional information
JC683	1937	Formerly WPW1001 converted in 1975
JC688	1925	Formerly Flat Wagon F308 converted in 1953
JC689	1925	Formerly Flat Wagon F309 converted in 1955
JC691	1931	Formerly Flat Wagon F312 converted in 1963

Track maintenance machines

Number Range	Type Code	Type	Date Introduced
Built by Plasser & Theurer			
PBT761–763†	VKR05	Tamper	1966
PBT764†	AL 250	Liner	1973
SC765	PLM07275	Tamper	1975
TMM771–773	PU0716	Tamper	1980

Built by Mercedes-Benz Unimog

TMM774 (A723 LNW) U1000		Track cleaner	1982
TMM775	—	Trailer	1982

† Stored awaiting disposal.

Below: There are a number of bogie flat wagons in service constructed by various manufacturers during 1931–66 for engineering department use, that are now up for retirement. No F366 illustrated was built in 1956 by Gloucester RC&W and was refurbished during 1983 by W. H. Davis & Son. The wagon has removable sides which clip over side stanchions and can carry a 30 ton cargo. It is fitted for air brake operation and has buck-eye couplers. *John Glover*

Bottom: For the transportation of rails, both the running and electric type, a fleet of wagons classified by LTE as RW are in operation; these are bogie vehicles which have a carrying capacity of 20 tons. Wagons of this type were constructed by Metro-Cammell, Gloucester RC&W and BR. No RW506 illustrated was introduced in 1965 and constructed by BR at Ashford works. Some of these vehicles are fitted with electric hoists whilst others have handrails for working on welded rail trains. *John Glover*

Below: Ballast is usually transported to engineering sites in hopper type wagons; two types are currently in operation—the four-wheeled wagon of 1935–65 vintage and the modern bogie type introduced from 1981. The upper illustration shows one of the four-wheeled vehicles, fitted with both central and side ballast chutes controlled by the wheels on the near end, surface height shackle couplers and tube height ward couplers being fitted. No HW403 as illustrated was built in 1935. The lower illustration shows the latest type of bogie hopper built in 1981 by W. H. Davis and has a carrying capacity of 30 tons. 22 of this design are in service and again both centre and side ballast chutes are fitted. These vehicles have shackle and buck-eye couplers. *Both: John Glover*

Above: There are currently nine brake vehicles in operation on the LTE system. Some of these are retained for special applications whilst others are used generally on engineers trains. No B558 illustrated is painted in maroon livery with full yellow ends and used for instrumentation with the brake test train, often being used with locomotive No 12 *Sarah Siddons*. This vehicle was built in 1935 by Hurst Nelson and is of the 20 ton type. *John Glover*

Below: Some brake vans have been converted to tube stock match wagons, primarily carried out to assist with the removal of withdrawn stock to breaker's yards. Match brake No B585 illustrated is coupled to a train of 1938 tube stock and was photographed at Toton en route to a Rotherham scrap dealer. This vehicle has yellow livery with red lettering and was built in 1965 by BR at Ashford works. Note the single air brake pipe attached to the buffer beam. *Colin J. Marsden*

Above: In early 1984 a fleet of eight personnel carriers were in service, used to transport staff engaged in engineering train operation. Cars PC850–PC856 are converted from pre-1938 stock trailers, and retain their original doors/windows. Three further cars Nos PC857–859 were introduced in 1980–81 converted from 1938 stock DMs. These are of different appearance and have all except four door windows on each side plated over. The illustration shows PC No 855 at Lillie Bridge depot painted in maroon livery. This vehicle was rebuilt from trailer No 7071. *LURS collection*

Above and right: This and the two following illustrations show the Tunnel Cleaning Train or TCC. It was constructed by Acton Works between 1972–77 and is a five-car formation numbered TCC1–5. Vehicles TCC1 and TCC5 are Driving Motor vehicles converted from 1938 tube stock DMs. These cars contain traction equipment for movement of the set to site, and in addition car TCC1 has a hydraulic drive unit used when the train is tunnel cleaning. Behind the driving position there is an operator's cabin from where the train is controlled when in use. Coupled to the driving cars are filter vehicles Nos TCC2 and TCC4 which unload dust drawn in from the middle nozzle car numbered TCC3. When in operation the train travels at only between ½–6mph. The above illustration shows the train from the TCC5 end, while the one right above shows the formation from the TCC1 end. Note the three high powered headlights mounted on the roof each end, which are used when cleaning is in progress. The final illustration on the lower right shows one of the DM vehicles under construction. *John Glover (2), LT News*

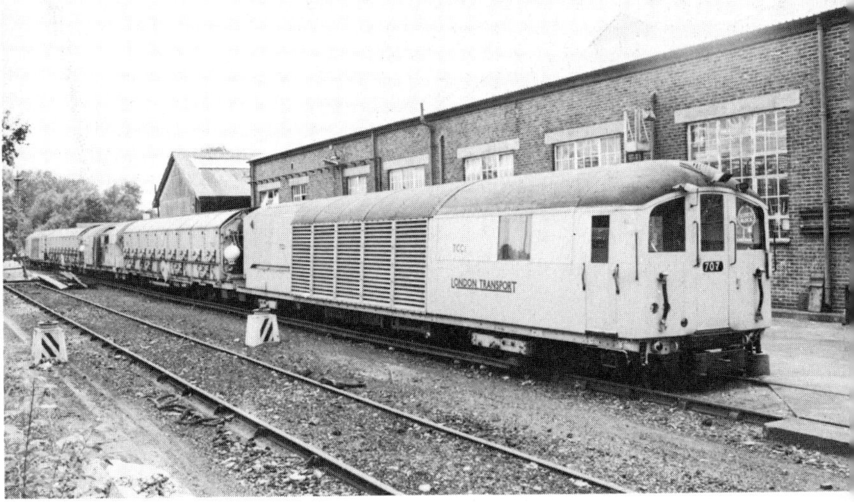
LONDON TRANSPORT
707

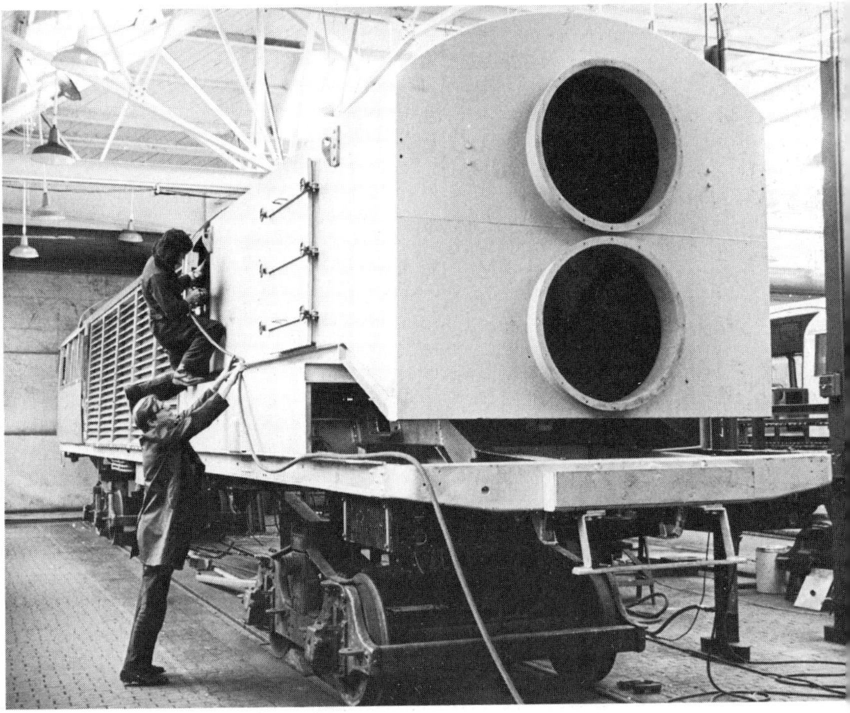

Top: Two rail grinding cars were introduced in 1956 rebuilt from pre-1938 tube stock and numbered RG802 and RG803. The cars carry grinding equipment and operate between a pair of pilot or ballast motor cars. During 1977–79 the cars were used in the leaf and rail cleaning train trying to solve the problem of lost adhesion during the leaf fall season. In July 1981 RG803 visited the SR and worked test trips between Kingston and Shepperton sandwiched between Pilot motor cars Nos L131/132. The train is seen here in the bay at Kingston. Both cars are out of service awaiting disposal. *Colin J. Marsden*

Above: A total of five permanent way cranes are in operation, the oldest one entering service in 1931 and the most modern in 1982. Jib runners usually work with the cranes and these are converted from former flat wagons. The crane illustrated No DEC617 is a Taylor Hubbard machine introduced in 1955, its jib rests on runner wagon No JC688 converted from flat wagon No F308. *LTE*

Above and below: These two illustrations show the oldest of the crane stock in service No C606, a Ransome & Rapier machine introduced in 1931 as a steam crane and converted for diesel operation by Cowans Sheldon Ltd in 1978. Buffing equipment on the crane consists of hinged buffers, shackle coupling, and through air pipes. The illustration below shows the match or jib runner for the crane, this was introduced in 1975 to replace an older withdrawn vehicle. Jib carrier No JC683 was converted from a bogie well wagon No WPW1001, coupling arrangements on this vehicle are hinged buffers, screw shackle coupling, control jumper socket and tube height Ward couplers. *Both: John Glover*

Left and below: There are six Plasser & Theurer tamping machines currently in operation; one type PLM07–275 for points and crossing work and five type PU07–16 machines suitable for straight track operation. These machines are similar to those in use on BR but are constructed to LT loading gauge. There are no buffers but Ward type couplers are provided. The illustration shows machine No 771 at Acton Works whilst the lower plate is of machine No 773, giving a display of its functions at Neasden Open Day on 24 April 1983. All machines are painted yellow. *Both: John Glover*

Above: A Unimog tractor/trailer combination was delivered at the end of 1982. The machine can operate on both roadways and rail tracks and is basically a lorry powered by a Mercedes Benz engine, hauling a trailer. The vehicle was ordered in connection with the battle against fallen leaves. The Unimog can traverse rail tracks where large quantities of leaves are known to fall and suck them up into a 16cu m tank in the trailer vehicle, leaves being collected by flexible nozzle heads between the tractor and trailer portion. Normally the Unimog is kept for rail transport but it can, if required, have the rail wheels lifted and is then able to work on public roadways within 20 minutes. The upper illustration shows the machine with its rail wheels in use, whilst the lower plate shows it in road transport mode. Livery is yellow and the number allocated is TMM774 (motor) and TMM775 (trailer). It also has the registration number of A723 NW. *Both: John Glover*

Waterloo & City

Waterloo and Bank

The 1½ miles Waterloo & City line was opened by the London & South Western Railway in 1898 to afford that company's passengers access to the City of London. It remains in the British Rail network today, and is part of the Southern Region. The original rolling stock was replaced from 1938, when the present cars were built:

Built by: English Electric, Preston

Car type:	DMBS	TS
Class No:	487	487
Length:	49ft 2in	49ft 2in
Height:	9ft 7in	9ft 7in
Width:	8ft 8in	8ft 8in
Seating:	40	52
Weight:	23 ton	19 ton
Car Nos:	S51–S62	S71–S86
Train formation:	Two or five car trains	

The normal formation is two motor cars sandwiching three trailers, an assembly which provides 236 seats and a (theoretical) additional standing capacity of 360. Using four trains, services operate every four minutes during the two peak hours, when half the daily 32,000 passenger journeys take place. The service interval lengthens to six minutes off-peak, and train formations may be reduced. On Saturdays, trains operate every 15 minutes until 13.30.

The line consists of two single track running tunnels of 12ft 1¾in diameter, increasing to 12ft 9in on the sharp curves to accommodate the end throw of the vehicles. At Bank there is a scissors crossover and trains use the two platforms alternately, but at Waterloo arriving and departing trains are kept separate; trains proceed between the platforms via the depot sidings where maintenance is also carried out. Access to and from the system, which is all underground, is provided by the Armstrong lift in the north sidings at Waterloo. This is needed to transfer cars to Selhurst depot, where wheelturning and overhauls are carried out.

Signalling dates from 1940 with signalboxes at both stations, although points and signals are automatically operated at Bank through time element relays coupled to the track circuits. Train stops are provided intermediately, and also in the terminal platforms at Bank. A 20mile/h speed restriction applies over much of the line, with 10mile/h over the junctions.

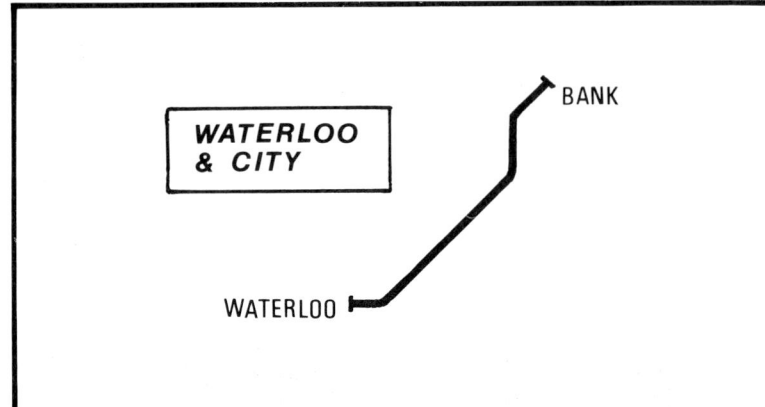

Passenger access to platforms is by staircases at Waterloo, but at Bank there is the choice of stairs or the travelator. Opened in 1960, the two travelators increased the capacity of the line by allowing quicker clearance of the platforms; they also offer prime advertising space, and many poster campaigns are designed to be read progressively from one end of the shaft to the other.

Trains are manned by driver and guard, and single manning could only be contemplated with replacement rolling stock. A system of stepback crews is employed; such is the volume of passengers that turnround times can only be achieved by having relief crews at Bank positioned ready to takeover incoming trains.

Above: A model on display at the London Transport Museum showing a cut-away of Bank station on the Waterloo & City line. *John Glover*

Below: Motive power for the Waterloo & City line is provided by 12 double cab motor cars, eight normally required for the advertised passenger service. All DM cars face the same direction ie: power equipment at Bank end. Behind the driving position at this end is an equipment room housing all power and auxiliary equipment. Cars Nos S51/52 stand coupled in the sidings at Waterloo. *Colin J. Marsden*

Above: For coupling between the DM vehicles a total of 14 Trailer vehicles are provided; 12 of these are required for the passenger services. Two pairs of double leaf sliding doors are on trailer vehicles but only one set of double and one single leaf door are provided on DM cars. Trailer No S71 is illustrated. *Colin J. Marsden*

Below: Waterloo & City line trains are formed of either two or five cars; usually five car trains are formed DM, T, T, T, DM. However as all the DM vehicles are double cab units two can be coupled together and operated as a power twin. This normally happens during off peak periods but normally not more than one two-car formation is used at one time. A five-car train stands at Waterloo with DM No S59 nearest to the camera. *John Glover*

Below: Although the Waterloo & City line has full depot facilities at Waterloo capable of undertaking quite major overhauls to stock, when classified overhauls are due these are undertaken by Selhurst depot. To transfer stock to Selhurst necessitates moving the required vehicle to the surface via the Armstrong lift at the Waterloo end of the line, and forming it into a special train marshalled between two match wagons. DM No S59 is seen inside Selhurst shop mounted on accommodation stands during August 1980. *John Glover*

Left: For a number of years the Waterloo & City line was host to electric locomotive No 75S, which was used in sidings at Waterloo to shunt wagons and unpowered stock. The loco was built in 1898 and used on the line until 1968 when the electrical equipment became obsolete and it was withdrawn and stored at Brighton until moved to the National Railway Museum at York in late 1977. The machine is now restored to chocolate livery as No 75S. It is seen here parked on the side of one of the turntables in the NRM during 1983. *Colin J. Marsden*

Isle of Wight

Ryde Pier Head–Brading–Shanklin

The present Isle of Wight rail service was inaugurated in 1967, being the electrified 8½ mile remnant of the formerly extensive (55½ route miles) island rail system.

Because of limited clearances in Ryde Tunnel, which is susceptible to flooding, and a generally confined structure gauge, choice of rolling stock was problematical. Finally, former London Transport Underground 'standard' stock was selected. At the present time, 37 cars are available for service, the oldest of which celebrated its diamond jubilee in 1984. The trains thus become, by a substantial margin, the oldest passenger rolling stock in regular revenue earning use in Britain.

Details are as follows:

Built by: Metro-Cammell, Union Car Co, Cammell Laird.
Class: 485 (4VEC), 486 (3TIS).
Unit Nos: 485.041–485.045, 486.031–486.035.

Car types:	DMBSO	TSO	DTSO
Length:	51ft 6in	49ft 9in	50ft 3in
Height:	9ft 6in	9ft 6in	9ft 6in
Width:	8ft 8in	8ft 8in	8ft 8in
Seating:	26	42	38
Weight:	29 tons	19 tons	17 tons
Car nos (range):	S1–S22	S41–S96	S26–S36
Train formation:	Four or seven cars		

The cars were modified for third-rail operation and overhauled at Acton Works, and then transferred to Stewarts Lane where they were painted and had luggage shelves fitted. Trials and crew training were carried out on the South Western Division. From Fratton, the cars were transported to Ryde on a Pickfords low loader, using the Portsmouth–Fishbourne car ferry. Two types of unit were formed, the four-car (4VEC) and three-car (3TIS) combining to form seven-car trains (VECTIS), the Roman name for the island. Some cosmetic refurbishment has recently been undertaken with the trains now being painted in blue and grey (Inter-City!) livery and reupholstered in London Transport moquette as used in the D and 1983 stock trains.

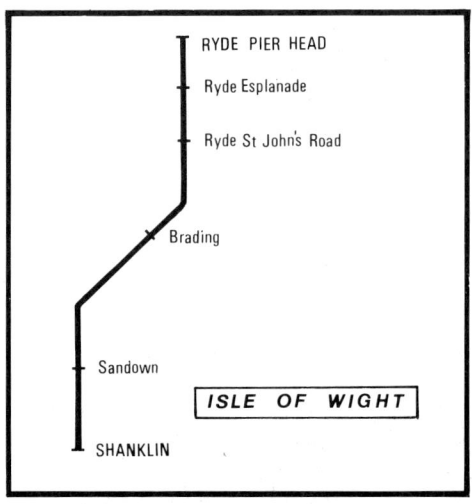

RYDE PIER HEAD
Ryde Esplanade
Ryde St John's Road
Brading
Sandown
SHANKLIN

ISLE OF WIGHT

The only double track sections are between Ryde Esplanade and Smallbrook (former junction for Cowes), and between Brading and Sandown. The timetable, which provides for up to three trains per hour on summer Saturdays, but dropping to hourly on winter Sundays, has to be fitted round these constraints. Normally, an additional train is confined to the second track between Esplanade and Pier Head, providing a local service between the town and the ferries.

Maintenance is carried out at St John's Road depot in the converted steam shed. The only other motive power is a British Rail Class 03 shunter No 97.804; this is used by the civil engineer together with a fleet of wagons. It can usually be found at Sandown when not in use.

Replacement policy for the rolling stock is undetermined, with the most likely candidates being the 1959/62 tube stock when this is displaced from its present duties from 1990 onwards. However, the underfloor equipment poses maintenance problems as Ryde Works is not equipped with pits, and exposure to sea spray on the pier might also have unfortunate effects!

Above: The former pre-1938 tube stock operating on the Isle of Wight is by far the oldest passenger stock operating in Britain. It is maintained to a high standard and provides the full rail passenger service on the Island. Usually trains are formed of seven coaches—one three-car and one four-car unit coupled together, but single four-car units are permitted to run on their own. 4VEC No 044 leads a seven-car formation out of Brading with a Shanklin–Ryde working in August 1980. *John Glover*

Below: Three types of vehicle are in operation: MBS (Motor Brake Second), TS (Trailer Second) and DTS (Driving Trailer Second). Four-car units are formed MBS, TS, TS, MBS, while three-car sets are formed DTS, TS, MBS. When the units first went to the Island they carried all blue livery with yellow ends; in the late 1970s several units were painted with grey doors and it is in this condition that we see a seven-car formation led by 3TIS No 034 approach Ryde St Johns. *John Glover*

Left: After a decision was made that no 'new' stock would be made available to the Isle of Wight for a considerable period, a light refurbishing programme was carried out on the majority of vehicles at Ryde Works. When cars emerged they were painted in Inter-City blue-grey livery and carried their six digit unit numbers below the non-driving window. Refurbished seven-car formation led by VEC No 485041 approaches Smallbrook Junction with the 17.39 Ryde–Shanklin on 13 June 1982. *Colin J. Marsden*

Below: During the rebuilding of stock for the Isle of Wight some seating was replaced by luggage racks as it was envisaged that a considerable number of holiday makers would make use of the line. The revised seating was MBS cars 26, TSO 42 and DTS 38, therefore a seven-car correctly formed train would carry 242 seated passengers with sufficient room for an equal number standing. Refurbished set '043 is pictured at Ryde St Johns whilst working the 11.37 Ryde Pier Head–Shanklin on 14 June 1983. *Colin J. Marsden*

Left: The front equipment of the VEC/TIS stock has altered very little. Air operated whistles are positioned to the left of the driver's window, main reservoir/brake pipes are nose mounted, and marker/tail lights are positioned under the non-driving window. Three jumper cable sockets are on the front just above buffing height, these are: (left–right) Control, Brake and Auxiliary. Ward type couplers are fitted. Set '043 approaches Brading with the 12.55 Ryde–Shanklin on 13 June 1982. *Colin J. Marsden*

Below: Car No S10 is allocated to the system as a spare and is used when a 'correct' car is undergoing maintenance. When the refurbishing programme was in progress it was used frequently. No unit number is carried by this vehicle but a stencil frame is positioned in the non-driving window where the unit number the car is in can be displayed. No S10 operating in unit 031 stands at Shanklin during 1982.
Colin J. Marsden

The Glasgow Underground

Buchanan Street–St Enoch–Govan–Hillhead–Buchanan Street (circular)

The Glasgow Underground was opened in 1896 as a cable hauled system; it was electrified with third-rail 600v dc in 1935 using the original rolling stock. The original track plan consisted of two concentric circles each 6½ miles long with no pointwork. Cars were raised to ground level for maintenance purposes by means of a hoist. The track gauge was 4ft only, and the tunnels 11ft in diameter, compared with 12ft in London. All 15 stations were equipped with centre island platforms leading to the persistent but unfounded story that this allowed Glasgow Corporation, who owned the system, not to paint the sides of the cars further from the platform edge as these could not be seen!

Approval for modernisation of the system was finally given in 1974. Closure to enable the work to be carried out was precipitated by a crack in a station roof in 1977; the system reopened to the public in 1980. Modernisation, under the control of Strathclyde Passenger Transport Executive, was thorough; among the more notable station works were the construction of side platforms at the busier locations to segregate 'inner' and 'outer' rail passengers, abandonment of Merkland Street station and its replacement by Partick for interchange with British Rail, installation of escalators at nine stations, and a travelator linking Buchanan Street with Queen Street BR. A ramp was provided to enable trains to reach Broomloan depot at Govan in the conventional manner so that service frequencies can be varied at different periods of the day, and to enable trains to be stabled in the depot at night rather than being left in the tunnels. New trains were provided as follows:

Built by: Metro-Cammell

Car type:	DM
Length:	41ft 3in
Height:	8ft 8in
Width:	7ft 8in
Seating per car:	34
Weight:	19.05 tons
Numbers:	101–133
Number of cars:	33, all single ended
Usual train formation:	Two or three-car units

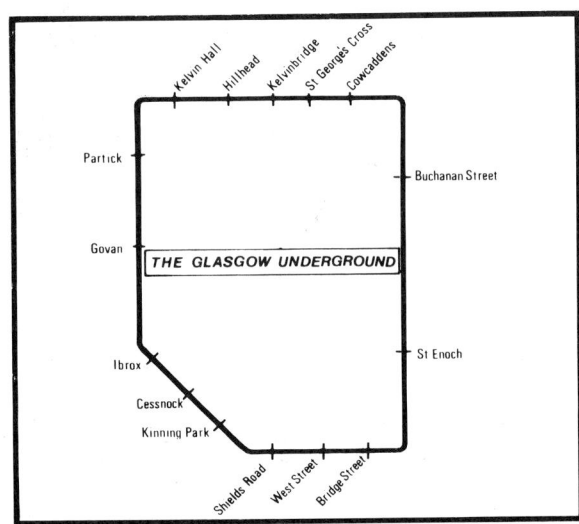

The maximum service speed is 33mile/h, and a complete circuit is achieved in 22 minutes, giving an average speed of 18mile/h. Since no passenger will usually travel more than half the circuit on the 'Clockwork Orange', average journey length is short at 1.8 miles. Present usage is 12 million passenger journeys per annum.

A form of Automatic Train Operation is used. Beacons mounted between the rails are interrogated by train borne equipment and up to ten command signals can be passed to the train. These include three separate speed limit commands, three braking commands, start-permit, and maximum speed commands. Trains are driven manually between the depot and the first station (Govan on the outer circle, Ibrox on the inner), but in normal automatic running the driver merely depresses the two 'start' buttons. There is also a conventional automatic block signalling system; any signal can be held at red by the train controllers for regulating purposes.

Battery and diesel locomotives are available for use on works trains.

Top: Two Greater Glasgow 'TransClyde' *Clockwork Orange* trains pass at Govan, to the west of the City. When built stations had central island platforms only but due to severe overcrowding some now have side platforms to assist the passenger flow. All trains on the system are formed of two or three identical cars capable of carrying 68/102 seated passengers, with space for an equal number standing. *John Glover*

Above: Frontal equipment on the stock consists of fully automatic couplings at buffing level controllable from the cab. Red rear indicators are carried on the edges of the buffing beam, while two headlights are fitted on the nose and either side of the front emergency door. Train reporting numbers are displayed in the driver's window. Train No 3 arrives at Buchanan Street, one of the stations reconstructed with one side platform. *John Glover*

101

Top: Interior of *Clockwork Orange* train. All cars are built by Metro-Cammell and of the same design. Seating is in longitudinal form and passenger access is by two double leaf sliding doors on each car. No opening windows are provided, forced air ventilation being fitted. The interior of car No 125 is shown. *John Glover*

Above: Driving cab layout. Trains usually operate on an automatic mode whereby the driver presses a start button and the train receives command signals from track borne equipment, in terms of acceleration, coasting, braking etc. However manual power control is fitted for movement between the depot at Broomloan and the running lines. In this view the communication system can be seen at the back, with brake, speed and general indications on the desk slope. Door controls and start buttons are positioned on the flat of the desk together with manual brake controls, master key position and emergency stop button. *John Glover*

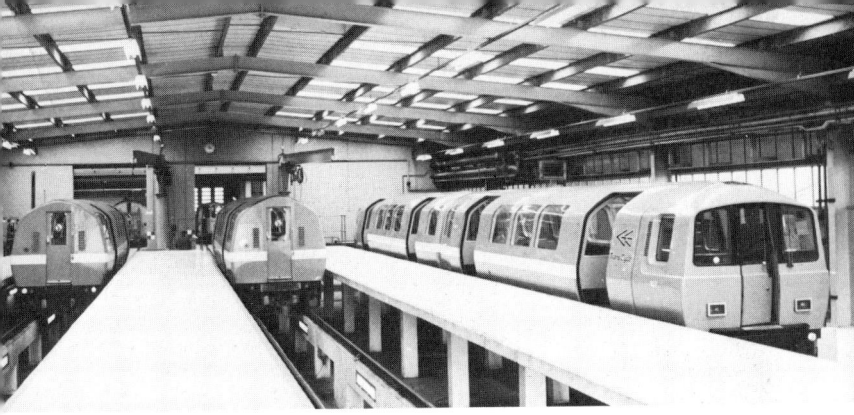

Above: Depot facilities for the 33 single cab cars is at Broomloan, near Govan, where all repairs are undertaken, ranging from routine cleaning to classified overhauls. Two cars stand with their inner ends nearest the camera, whilst a complete set stands on the right. Photographed on 3 July 1981.
John Glover

Below: The present stock on the Strathclyde underground commenced operation in 1980, however the line first opened in 1896 as a cable hauled system, and later converted to 600v dc third-rail operation using original stock rebuilt for electric operation. Up to the time the line was closed for rebuilding in 1977, stock was hoisted to ground level for storage and maintenance. This photograph taken several years ago shows car No 15 being lowered back to the underground system from the carriage sheds.
Author's collection

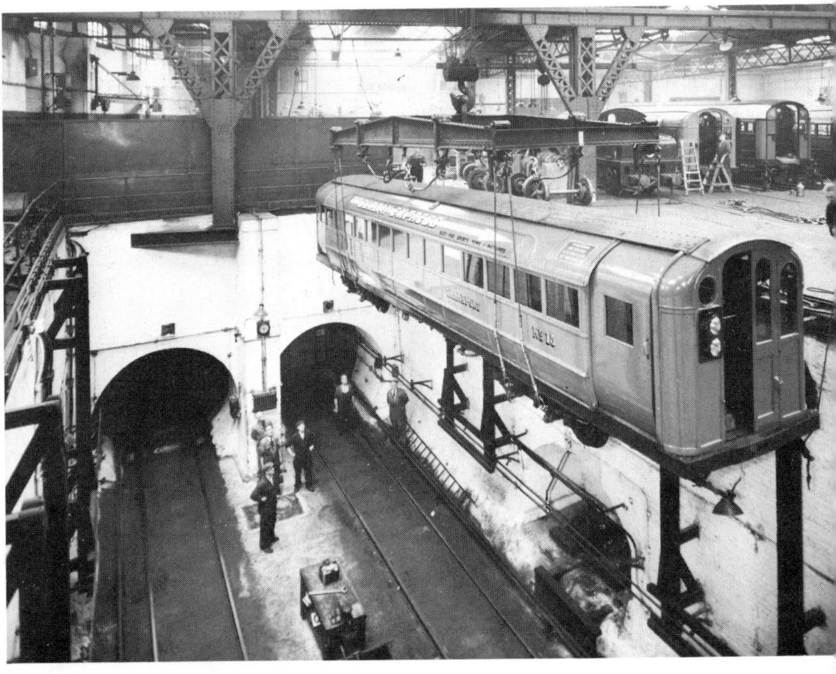

Tyne & Wear Metro

South Shields–Monument–South Gosforth–Tynemouth–Monument–St James, with a branch from South Gosforth to Bank Foot.

The Tyne & Wear Metro had its origins in the Tyne Wear Plan of the late 1960s. This document proposed 'significant investment in a public transport system with its own right of way based on the current railway, with renewal and upgrading of lines and stations and improvements in central area accessibility'.

The first section of the 1,500v dc Metro was opened in August 1980 between Tynemouth and Haymarket. Subsequent extensions of operation followed, with the system being completed to South Shields in 1984. Its total route length is 35 miles, of which 27 miles are converted British Rail suburban routes. The eight miles of new construction, about half of which is underground, is to provide accessibility to central Newcastle and Gateshead and to improve the cross-Tyne link. This latter is afforded by the Queen Elizabeth II bridge. A major realignment in Byker traverses the 18 span Ouseburn viaduct, a new route in South Shields taps a major residential area, and a freight only route has been reopened to passengers from South Gosforth to Bank Foot. A connection for stock working purposes is provided between West Jesmond and Manors. Additional stations are now under construction at Kingston Park and Pelaw.

All services are operated by the fleet of Metrocars, details as follows:

Built by: Metro-Cammell
Car type: Six axle twin articulated units
Length: 91ft 3in
Height: 11ft 4in
Width: 8ft 8in
Seating per unit: 84
Weight: 38.3 tons
Numbers: 4001–4090*
Number of units: 90
Usual train formation: Two units

* Cars Nos 4001/2 are prototypes with detail differences, and are at present stored out of use.

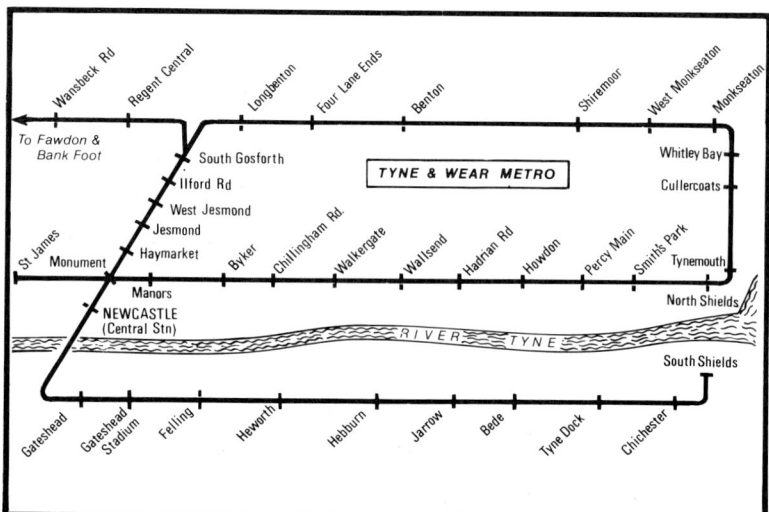

Above: Prior to large investment being placed for the development of rolling stock for the Tyne & Wear Metro system, Metro-Cammell built prototype two-coach articulated sets Nos 4001/2. These units operated on the test track where points, crossings and a small station were built. These units differ from the type ordered in many ways and if this and the other illustrations are compared the differences become obvious. One of the requirements for this line was for single man operation and for this reason television cameras were provided at all stations with a monitor visible to the driver. This equipment can be seen in this illustration. *Department of Trade & Industry*

There are four Metrolines:

Metroline 1	Colour Green	Bank Foot and South Shields
Metroline 2	Colour Red	Benton and Heworth
Metroline 3	Colour Yellow	St James and Heworth
Metroline 4	Colour Blue	St James and North Shields

On each line there is a train every 10 minutes during the working day. Together they provide three trains every ten minutes between South Gosforth and Heworth, and every five minutes between North Shields and St James. The system is double track throughout, except for a short section at the approach to Bank Foot, and part of the South Shields branch beyond Heworth. A maximum of 34 trains each consisting of two units is required to provide the service, reducing to 24 (evenings and Sundays) and 12 (Sunday early morning).

Maximum service speed of a Metrotrain is 50mile/h. Trains are one man operated and the 'one third' cabs allow passengers a forward view unparalleled elsewhere in the UK. Trains are driven manually, and there is an automatic block signalling system.

The Metro Control Centre is at South Gosforth station. Train drivers 'dial' their route themselves by initiating a coding device in the cab before starting their journey, which will result in automatic route setting at junctions. The system controller can however override any routes thus set up. The station controller monitors the system through CCTV cameras and checks remotely for malfunctions of station equipment such as ticket machines, escalators etc. Stations are unstaffed, but there is a squad of mobile inspectors. The power controller's duties are to ensure secure power supplies and to maintain electrical safety. There is a three channel radio system for contact between controllers, trainmen, operating and maintenance staff, as well as a comprehensive public address system.

All Metrocars are based at the Gosforth Traction Maintenance Depot, which also houses the four 427hp 0-6-0 diesel-electric shunters built by Brush for works trains.

Top: All Tyne & Wear Metro cars are maintained at their depot at South Gosforth, situated in the triangle of lines between South Gosforth, Regent Centre and Longbenton. Front end equipment of cars consists of automatic 'tightlock' couplers, head lights and rear tail indicators. Destination blinds are positioned above the full width front window, and car numbers usually appear on the nose end above the Tyne & Wear Metro sign. Car No 4054 departs from the depot during 1980. *John Glover*

Above: Passenger access to cars is by twin 'plug' type doors, seen here in the open position. These are controlled by the train operator (driver) and prior to closing an alarm is given to warn passengers to stand clear. Livery of this stock is orange base and cream upper. Platforms at most stations have been constructed to enable flat access from platform to car, as seen here at Gateshead. *John Glover*

Above: Interior of passenger car with seating arranged in the 2+2 transverse arrangement. The driving position (at the far end of the car shown) occupies only one-third of the total car width, the other area being available to passengers. Above the side windows are advertisement panels together with a route map of the line. By each door position on a post in the centre of the car is an emergency brake button which when pressed operates one of the braking wires running throughout the train and fully applies the brakes. The equipment has to be reset by the driver before the train can continue its journey. *John Glover*

Below: For construction and maintenance of the line Brush Traction (BEM) produced four 427hp 0-6-0 diesel electric locomotives numbered WL1–4. These are single cab units fitted with standard buffing gear but dual couplings, enabling them to be coupled to conventional stock and Tyne & Wear Metro cars. Through air connections are provided. No WL1 is seen at Whitley Bay with a two vehicle engineer's train on 17 April 1980. *John Glover*

Docklands Light Railway

Tower Hill (Minories) to Island Gardens (Isle of Dogs), with a branch to Stratford.
The Docklands Light Railway is the joint responsibility of London Regional Transport and the London Docklands Development Corporation. Government support for the new railway was announced in 1982, and it is the intention that the initial system should be operational by July 1987. The railway, by providing a greatly enhanced transport service, is part of the overall effort aimed at regenerating London's derelict dockland area. It is to be built by a consortium of GEC and John Mowlem.

Much of the railway, which will be on segregated rights of way throughout, will be constructed on brick built arches formerly used by British Rail services, some of which have been abandoned for many years. Although basically double track, single track will be used approaching both the Island Gardens and Stratford termini. Sixteen stations will serve the seven and a half route miles, with the single depot situated at North Quay.

Eleven 9ft 6in twin articulated standard gauge vehicle units of about 8ft 6in wide with 80 seats and space for an additional 120 standing passengers will provide the service. Third rail current collection will be used. A sophisticated control system will result in automatic operation; doors will be opened by passengers, but departure will be initiated by a staff member who will also be on board to assist passengers. Stations will be unstaffed.

Service levels will be determined by the progress made in developing the area. Initially, there will be a 7½ minute frequency on each of the Tower Hill–Island Gardens and Stratford–Island Gardens routes.

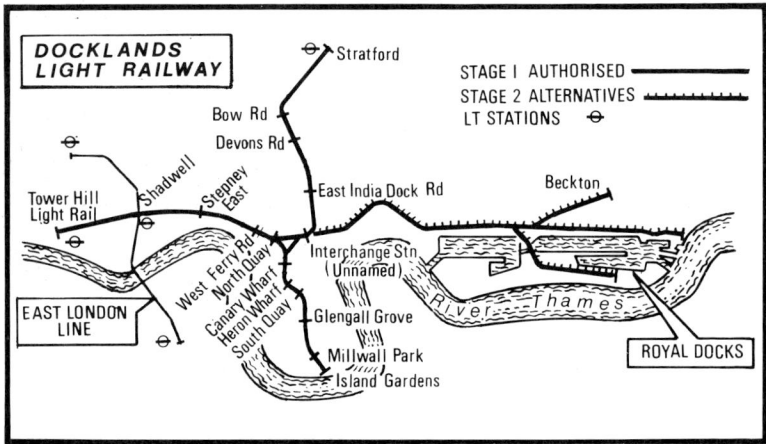

Preserved Vehicles

Various items of London Underground rolling stock have been preserved, particularly at the London Transport Museum in Covent Garden. Opened in 1979, this representative collection traces the history of London Transport and its predecessors. Other 'officially' preserved vehicles include a Q23 car by the Gloucester Railway Carriage & Wagon Co, whilst the Science Museum, London, exhibits a 1927 tube motor car and an original City & South London Railway electric locomotive. Some vehicles are in the hands of preservation societies, notably former Metropolitan coaching stock, and also six ex-BR '57xx' 0-6-0PT locomotives which have mostly reverted to Great Western livery.

Above: This little 0-4-0 Aveling Porter machine entered service in January 1872 on the Wooton Tramway, a 6½-mile long branch from Quainton Road to Brill. Before the turn of the century it was replaced by a more powerful locomotive and sold to a brickworks in Northamptonshire where it worked until 1940. After being dumped in a derelict state for some 10 years it was saved by the Industrial Locomotive Society and stored at Neasden depot from where it went on display at Clapham Transport Museum, later Syon Park Museum, and is presently on display at Covent Garden LT Museum. *John Glover*

Below left: Metropolitan Railway No 23 was built in 1866 by Beyer Peacock of Manchester for use on the Metropolitan & District Railway 'cut and cover' lines, and due to it being mainly used in confined spaces steam condensing gear was fitted. This locomotive together with many others of the same design, remained in service until 1905 when electric traction took over. After being made redundant the machine was transferred to the service fleet where it operated engineers and departmental trains until 1948. It is now restored to near original condition and on display at Covent Garden. *John Glover*

Above: Metropolitan Railway milk van No 3 was built in 1896 by Birmingham RC&W Ltd as a van to carry milk churns on the rear of passenger trains, having a carrying capacity of 3 tons. After the vehicle was taken over by the LPTB in 1933 it became a goods brake van but was later saved from scrap and restored to original condition in the 1960s. It was first placed on display at Clapham Transport Museum but can now be seen at Covent Garden. *John Glover*

Below: Metropolitan Railway coach No 400 was constructed in 1900 by the Metropolitan works at Neasden as one of a fleet of bogie vehicles for use on the Metropolitan Railway. In 1921 it was rebuilt as a driving trailer for use with 'W' stock formations. The majority of coaches were scrapped around 1940 but six were retained for push-pull operation on the Chesham branch. No 400 was one of these and remained in service until 1961 when it was replaced by emu formations. No 400, by now numbered 519, was first stored at Neasden, and later at the Brighton Pullman shed, emerging in 1976 when it was returned to LT for restoration and display at the Covent Garden Museum. *John Glover*

Left: Regretfully only parts of some vehicles have been retained, and this applies to the exhibit of *gate* stock introduced between 1900–07. The portion on display comes from an Hungarian car built for the Piccadilly line. After its useful passenger service the vehicle was taken to Acton works where it entered departmental service. Eventually the vehicle was 'sectioned' and the gate end exhibited at Covent Garden Museum. The rear gate equipment has now been fully restored and clearly shows how the equipment operated. *John Glover*

Above: Q23 stock Motor car No 4248. This exhibit represents a typical clerestory roofed vehicle used on all underground lines from their electrification. The car shown was constructed in 1923 to replace some original vehicles in use on the District line. Comparatively, little alteration has been carried out in the design and layout of equipment on surface stock from this to vehicles presently in use. On the right the rear end of the City & South London driving car can be seen. *John Glover*

Above: 1938 stock DM No 11182. 1938 tube stock was introduced for use on the Northern and Bakerloo lines and examples of this type were still in operation in the spring of 1984 on the Bakerloo line. The vehicle has been restored to its 1950s appearance and is a worthy exhibit in the Museum as it represents the first of the conventional tube passenger vehicles built to have underslung power, traction and control equipment; hitherto the equipment had been carried in a compartment behind the driver. *John Glover*

Below: Q stock trailer No 08063 is preserved by the London Underground Railway Society. The vehicle was first preserved at the Ashford Steam Centre but from 1979 has been kept in London, first at Ruislip depot and more recently at Ealing Common depot. The vehicle is restored (one side and both ends) to Underground red livery with gold numbering and London Transport insignia. The vehicle was photographed at Acton Works Open Day on 2 July 1983. *John Glover*